PRAISE FOR

FLY, COLTON, FLY

"*Fly, Colton, Fly* reveals much about the Jesse James of the Facebook age—and our fascination with imaginative crooks eluding maladroit cops. Indispensable for anyone interested in the Barefoot Bandit."

—Rinker Buck, Author of *Flight of Passage*

"Every now and then, a criminal comes along who flouts the law with such daring and dash that he is elevated to the ranks of rebel folk hero. Colton Harris-Moore is the latest figure to enter the ranks of these legendary lawbreakers. In this fleet and propulsive account, Jackson Holtz tells the story of this latter-day Jesse James in a style best suited to its subject—with enormous panache."

—Harold Schechter, Author of *Killer Colt: Murder, Disgrace, and the Making of an American Legend*

Tacoma
OLYMPIA
Aberdeen
Chehalis
South Bend

FLY, COLTON, FLY

THE TRUE STORY OF THE BAREFOOT BANDIT

Jackson Holtz

New American Library

New American Library
Published by New American Library, a division of
Penguin Group (USA) Inc., 375 Hudson Street,
New York, New York 10014, USA
Penguin Group (Canada), 90 Eglinton Avenue East, Suite 700, Toronto,
Ontario M4P 2Y3, Canada (a division of Pearson Penguin Canada Inc.)
Penguin Books Ltd., 80 Strand, London WC2R 0RL, England
Penguin Ireland, 25 St. Stephen's Green, Dublin 2,
Ireland (a division of Penguin Books Ltd.)
Penguin Group (Australia), 250 Camberwell Road, Camberwell, Victoria 3124,
Australia (a division of Pearson Australia Group Pty. Ltd.)
Penguin Books India Pvt. Ltd., 11 Community Centre, Panchsheel Park,
New Delhi - 110 017, India
Penguin Group (NZ), 67 Apollo Drive, Rosedale, North Shore 0632,
New Zealand (a division of Pearson New Zealand Ltd.)
Penguin Books (South Africa) (Pty.) Ltd., 24 Sturdee Avenue,
Rosebank, Johannesburg 2196, South Africa

Penguin Books Ltd., Registered Offices:
80 Strand, London WC2R 0RL, England

First published by New American Library,
a division of Penguin Group (USA) Inc.

First Printing, April 2011
10 9 8 7 6 5 4 3 2 1

Maps by Judy Stanley, *Herald of Everett* graphic artist

LIBRARY OF CONGRESS CATALOGING-IN-PUBLICATION DATA:

Holtz, Jackson.
Fly, Cotton, fly: the story of the Barefoot Bandit/Jackson Holtz.
p. cm.
ISBN 978-0-451-23508-4
1. Harris-Moore, Colton. 2. Thieves—United States—Biography. 3. Criminals—United States—Biography. I. Title.
HV6653.H37H65 2011
364.16'2092—dc22 2010051929
[B]

Set in Janson Text
Designed by Spring Hoteling

Printed in the United States of America

FOR JEREMY

CONTENTS

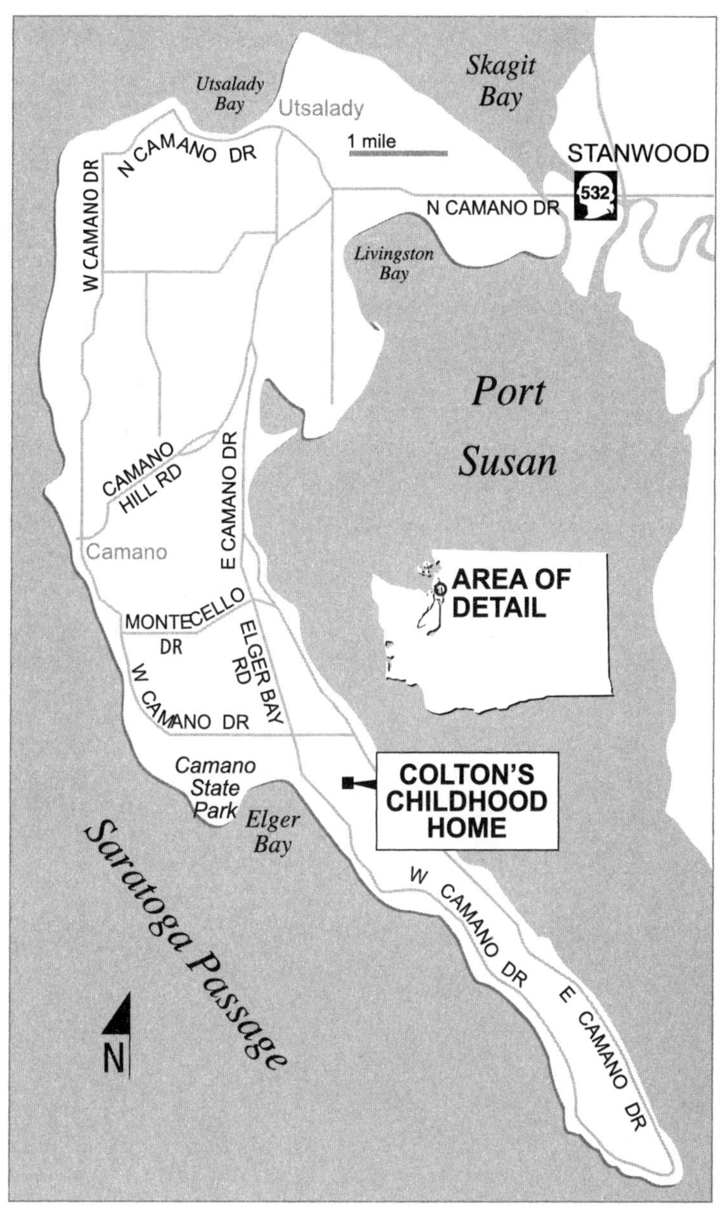

By Judy Stanley, Herald Graphic Artist

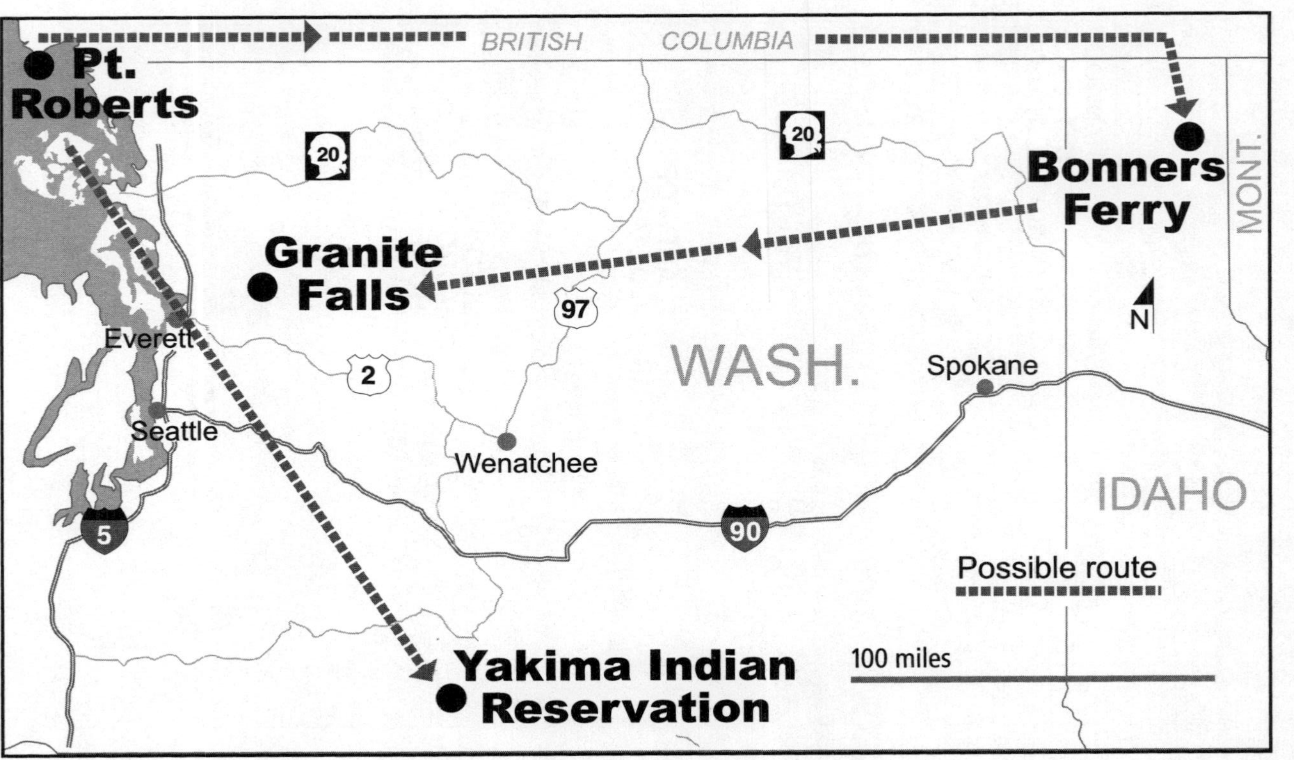

By Judy Stanley, Herald Graphic Artist

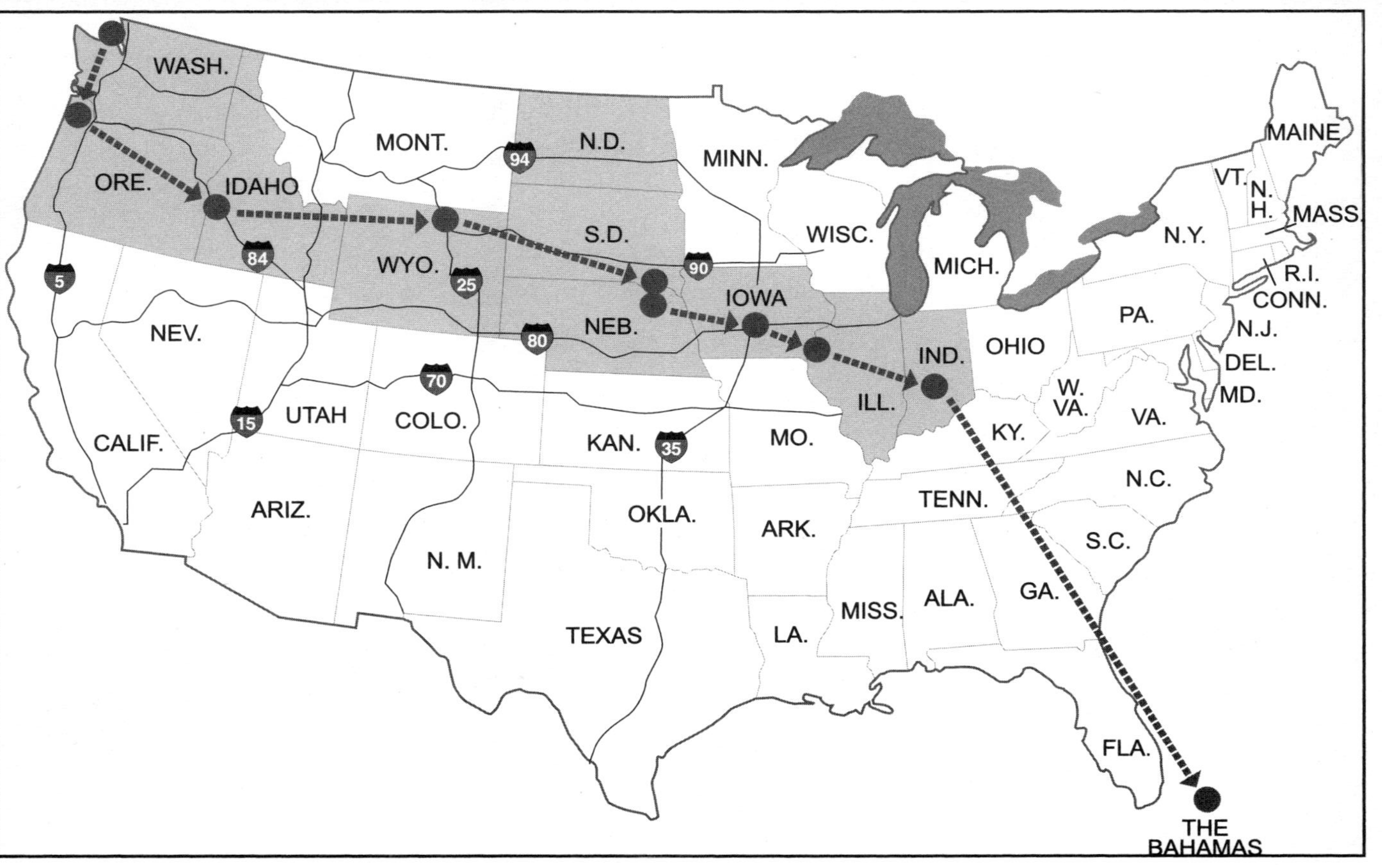

By Judy Stanley, Herald Graphic Artist

COLTON HARRIS-MOORE TIMELINE

March 22, 1991—Colton is born by cesarean section. His birth father leaves when he's a toddler and his stepdad dies when Colton is ten, about the same time his serious behavior problems are first documented. He's arrested the same year for theft. By fifteen he has a long rap sheet and is well known by local police. He's suspected of breaking into empty vacation homes and fleeing arrest by running into the woods.

February 2007—After six months on the run from police, Colton is arrested in connection with several burglaries and thefts. He's sentenced to three years in juvenile lockup.

April 22, 2008—Colton escapes Griffin Home, a halfway house for troubled adolescents near Seattle.

July 18, 2008—Colton crashes a stolen Mercedes into a propane tank behind the Elger Bay Grocery on Camano Island. Sheriff's deputies find a stash of stolen property in the car, including a camera with several self-portraits of Colton.

November 12, 2008—A Cessna airplane is stolen from Orcas Island and crashes near Yakima. Police don't make the connection to Colton until a second plane is stolen nearly a year later.

September 8, 2009—The Island Market on Orcas Island is

burglarized and an ATM vandalized. DNA tests link Colton to the crime.

September 22, 2009—A series of crimes, including a stolen plane from Friday Harbor, a missing boat from Orcas Island and a luxury car in Vancouver, lead police to suspect he's headed east through British Columbia.

September 29, 2009—A plane is taken from Bonners Ferry, Idaho. On October 1, a logger discovers the wreckage near Granite Falls, Washington. A shot is fired at a deputy investigating a campsite near the plane crash. Barefoot prints are found.

October 9, 2009—A Colton Harris-Moore Facebook fan page is launched. Soon thousands are following his exploits online.

December 11, 2009—Federal prosecutors secretly charge Colton with the Idaho plane theft.

February 11, 2010—Another stolen plane lands on Orcas Island. In the nearby town of Eastsound, a grocery store is burglarized and somebody draws thirty-nine barefoot prints on the floor.

May 15, 2010—Colton is seen on video surveillance at a Lopez Island marina where a boat is later taken. A trail of stolen boats and cars leads officials to believe that Colton is headed south toward Oregon.

May 29, 2010—An Everett bounty hunter joins the effort to catch Colton.

June 1, 2010—Colton sails the *Fat Cat*, a fishing boat, across the Columbia River from Ilwaco, Washington, to Warrenton, Oregon. He sets off from there on a 2,000-mile joyride across eight states.

June 2010—Colton is suspected of stealing cars and breaking into airports, homes and businesses in Oregon, Idaho, Wyoming, South Dakota, Nebraska, Iowa, Illinois and Indiana.

July 4, 2010—A top-of-the-line single-engine Cessna is taken from an airport in Bloomington, Indiana, and found crashed off the coast of the Bahamas. Colton is the prime suspect.

July 6, 2010—The FBI declares Colton an international fugitive and offers a $10,000 reward for his arrest. Wanted posters are distributed in the Bahamas.

July 11, 2010—Colton is arrested before dawn off Harbour Island. He tries to flee in a stolen boat but runs aground on a sandbar. Police shoot out the boat's twin outboards. Colton pleads guilty in a Bahamian court to entering the country illegally and is deported to Miami before being returned to Seattle.

November 10, 2010—A federal grand jury hands down a five-count indictment linking Colton to a multi-state crime spree including two plane thefts, a boat theft and weapons charges.

November 18, 2010—Colton enters a not guilty plea to all counts. His lawyer announces hopes of a plea arrangement. Colton still faces a dozen state charges in two Washington counties and in Nebraska.

AUTHOR'S NOTE

Colton Harris-Moore sat alone at the Federal Detention Center in Sea-Tac, Washington, awaiting trial as this book was being written. Like any other person who's been arrested, Colton is innocent until proven guilty. There are allegations that he committed more than eighty crimes, many of them felonies and some violations of federal law. There may never be a trial in this case; his lawyers may determine that the best course of action is to enter guilty pleas and hope the judge imposes a lenient sentence. The government likely has overwhelming evidence to convince a jury of Colton's alleged crimes.

It's worth noting that he was a convicted felon at fifteen and the crimes he committed until his April 2008 escape from a halfway house all have been adjudicated.

Much of the material in this book is based on allegations that had not been proven at the time the book went to print. At press time, Colton faced more than a dozen charges in state courts and a five-count federal indictment. The legal system was still gearing up for Colton's day in court. He had not been convicted of any crime in this country since 2007.

In several scenes in this book Colton's behavior is described as if it truly happened. Truth, in this case, is hard to find. As one cop told me, "There are facts and provable facts." For Colton, there are many facts, and it's hard to know how many can be proven. The only person who really knows what happened is Colton. Whether he'll ever tell us a believable account is an open question.

INTRODUCTION

When Island County sheriff Mark Brown announced in January 2007 that his department was looking for a fifteen-year-old serial burglar, the news caught my attention. It was the first time I'd heard of Colton Harris-Moore. I was the cops reporter at the *Herald* of Everett, Washington. Part of my beat coverage included writing about crimes in both Snohomish and Island counties, the communities just north of Seattle where Colton grew up.

Property crimes typically don't make news unless there's a twist that helps them rise above the daily reports of burglaries and thefts. The sheriff's case of a six-month burglary spree pinned to a lanky teenager rightly earned its way into the *Herald*. At the time, Sheriff Brown feared Colton and his then-accomplice, Harley Davidson Ironwing, were taking increasingly dangerous risks. Deputies worried the suspects were armed. The sheriff printed wanted posters featuring both boys' mug shots and urged local residents to lock their homes.

Colton was suspected of breaking into vacation homes on Camano Island, then sprinting off into the dense woods to escape the cops, the sheriff said. Locals reported rumors that this Colton had some peculiar traits: he often went barefoot, ran faster than any cop and sometimes even lived in the trees. Local television news stations sent crews to scour the island for hints of the tall, lanky teen burglar.

I grabbed my reporter's notebook and made the drive from Everett to south Camano Island. I met many people I would speak to over and over again during the next three years. Josh Flickner, the young manager of the Elger Bay Grocery. Mark Brown, the newly elected sheriff, and his detective, Ed Wallace. I'd have the first of dozens of conversations with Pam Kohler, Colton's mother.

As quickly as Colton's story broke, the chapter came to a close. On February 9, 2007, I was enjoying dinner out in Seattle, when the call came that Colton was arrested. My editor and I scrambled to change a story already set to run in Saturday's paper. That Monday I attended a brief bail hearing in Coupeville and got my first in-person glimpse of Colton Harris-Moore. It seemed to me and others that Colton's fifteen minutes of infamy were over. Like so many other crime stories that came and went, I believed Colton would capture headlines for a few days, and then fade.

We were wrong.

On April 22, 2008, Sheriff Brown contacted the *Herald* again. The slippery teen burglar that Brown and his department worked so hard to capture had escaped, crawling out the window of a halfway house in a Seattle suburb. Colton's greatest criminal feats and his flight into American history were just beginning.

This is the tale of the "Barefoot Bandit," the people in his life, his victims and his criminal adventures. The story follows his upbringing and his exploits. He started out stealing to survive and went on to steal for pleasure. His thefts grew from taking frozen pizzas to fancy electronics to cars and, despite no formal flight training, airplanes. He went on a two-year, nine-state crime spree, breaking into dozens of homes and businesses, and was often seen running away barefoot. He racked up more than three million dollars' worth of stolen or damaged property, including a high-end private plane he flew from Indiana to the Bahamas.

If he had been the subject of one massive manhunt on a small island and escaped, Colton could have earned some pride in beating law enforcement. He went beyond that. Police, FBI, Homeland Security and the U.S. Coast Guard used the latest investigative techniques to try to pin down the elusive teenager time and again. Colton always slipped away.

A colorful cast of characters surrounded the Barefoot Bandit. Pam Kohler, his mother, is a heavy drinker who delivered one outrageous comment after another in media interviews. Harley Davidson Ironwing has a bigger-than-life name for a two-bit criminal. Harley claimed he was Colton's criminal mentor. Navigating among their lies are slivers of truth that help give shape to Colton's story. There are his victims, including numerous families on Camano Island, where Colton grew up; business owners in Eastsound on Orcas Island; and people like John Miller, the beer distributor whose plane was stolen from a hangar in Indiana and crashed off the Bahamas. There's Zack Sestak, a young writer who started a Facebook fan page praising Colton, as well as a mysterious blogger who created a counterpoint, an anti-Colton Web page. There's Mike Rocha, the bounty hunter who claimed he would do what police hadn't been able to do—catch Colton. And there are all the many police officers who risked their lives to bring an end to Colton's joyrides.

One person you will not hear from directly: Colton Harris-Moore did not respond to my requests for interviews. His lawyer provided some glimpses into Colton's life on the run, but his comments must be taken in the context of a pending criminal case. Colton had plenty of opportunity to share his thoughts. If Osama bin Laden can post a video on the Internet from a cave in the Pakistani mountains, Colton could have blogged from a tent on the San Juan Islands. Colton kept his silence, save for the few messages he left behind—one in chalk on a grocery store floor, another a note left with one hundred dollars in cash dropped off at a veterinary clinic.

Instead, Colton participated in what one expert described as a very social kind of lawbreaking. His burglaries were, in effect, his Twitter postings. His planes thefts were his blog postings. Colton may not have had the time or inclination to update a Facebook page, but thousands of his online followers posted instead and cheered for him at every turn. He became the "Trickster," a barefooted, oversized Bart Simpson, whose games were a series of felonies. Colton became the first outlaw folk hero of the Internet age. What started as a neighborhood nuisance for Camano Island became a problem for the nation. CNN started covering Colton's crimes. *Time* magazine named him "America's Most Wanted Teen Bandit." His fate became fodder for Fox News.

Colton stole identities and used them to create his own sense of place in the world. While other boys his age were beginning to date, study for college entrance exams and work odd jobs, Colton was refining a practiced pattern of burglary and theft.

He did all this as a fugitive. Operating in mostly remote areas with small police forces, Colton outran law enforcement, mocking them along the way. Several times the cops turned up the heat, deploying the most sophisticated equipment available, to stop the Barefoot Bandit's odyssey. Sometimes he lurked nearby, watching the cops search. Other times he ran and ran.

INTRODUCTION

Colton was a serial burglar, a thief, a troubled kid whose extraordinary bravado landed him on the front pages of newspapers around the country. By the time he was arrested, barefoot and stuck on a sandbar in the Bahamas thousands of miles from home, Colton had captured fame. He went from being a young man from Camano Island with few prospects to being the Barefoot Bandit, an internationally known renegade. As this book went to print, he was a jailed nineteen-year-old facing a litany of federal and state charges, and the possibility of years, maybe decades, in prison. He soared at altitudes typically reserved for people who spend years training to be pilots and he reached great heights of infamy. He was abused and he fought back, waging a game with law enforcement that ended in a hailstorm of bullets in another country. He barged into many lives, stole from hundreds of people and frightened thousands more who lived on his flight path and in his territories. Colton also inspired, by thrilling a part not all of us will admit: sometimes it feels good to root for the bad guy. For a little while, that guy, the Barefoot Bandit, was winning, and we cheered him on: "Fly, Colton, Fly!"

FLY, COLTON, FLY

PART ONE

CHILDHOOD

CHAPTER ONE

For sixty years the Mark Clark Bridge had spanned the shallow tidal waters of Davis Slough between Stanwood and Camano Island. Built in 1949 and named for a World War II general, the bridge provided the only access to this remote community.

In earlier days, a swing bridge connected the island to the rest of western Washington. Bert Lawson was the first bridge tender and he lived with his family in a little house on the east end of the bridge, the mainland side. He kept a keen eye open for steamers and listened for the blast of their horns. As a boat approached, Lawson would swing the bridge open to let the vessels pass. The Mark Clark put Lawson out of business. The bridge stayed open until August 17, 2010, when it was replaced by the Camano Gateway Bridge, a utilitarian span built to better carry the thousands of cars and trucks that cross it daily. A month later, the Mark Clark was demolished.

The shift from one concrete roadway to another was met with enthusiasm but didn't much change the lives of the island's fourteen thousand permanent residents. For the most part, their routines stayed intact, save for perhaps fewer traffic jams when the bridge was closed down due to a car wreck.

Since the new bridge opened, Camano Island's most infamous resident had yet to cross it. Colton Harris-Moore, the boy who forced islanders to lock their doors and to fear the quiet rustle of leaves in the woods, was arrested weeks before the Mark Clark closed. He was in a secure federal detention center as summer changed to fall and the persistent rains returned to western Washington.

The Mark Clark was never much of an obstacle for Colton. He made his way on and off Camano Island with ease. Unlike the more exclusive San Juan Islands, a Washington archipelago reached only by ferry, private boat or plane, Camano Island makes a more accessible weekend vacation destination. In the summer, the island population swells to around twenty thousand as people flee the city suburbs, or return from winter homes in Arizona and Southern California.

Like the other islands in Puget Sound, Camano is awash in green and often wrapped in a misty cold and wet fog. If you're traveling by water, the islands emerge silhouetted against a monotone gray shroud. In the fall and winter, strong storms blow in off the Strait of Juan de Fuca and rip down trees, cluttering the roads with broken branches and pine needles. The wind and currents litter the miles of beaches with giant logs of driftwood. Whole tree trunks meet the tide. If the root ball is intact, it means the tree fell victim to a storm and was hurled downriver. A smooth cut at the end of the log means a logger took down the timber and the log escaped a raft or boom as the wood made its way to a mill.

Camano Island is a mostly quiet community filled with its own peculiar set of artists, retirees and people who prefer the privacy and silence the woods can offer. Camano is home to the Crochet Liberation Front, a group of crafters whose radical notion is to seek global domination with needle and stitch. Painters and glassmakers seek refuge here along with aging hippies, some of whom make up the South End String Band. During Colton's spree, the jug band wrote a ditty chronicling the teen's progress. The comical video, complete with reenactments of burglaries, was posted on YouTube and has attracted thousands of viewers. One man created pictorial spoofs of Colton that are displayed at the Tyee Grocery, a tiny general store on Camano's far south end.

Most of the time this is a peaceful place. It's an end-of-the-road community. Homes were built along the shoreline and down long, winding dirt driveways, purposefully isolated from neighbors. The wildlife is abundant. Salmon spawn in the tributaries. Bald eagles nest in the tall trees. Deer run through the thick woods. Once in a while a black bear wanders onto the island and into backyards. The bears are drawn to human habitats, especially in the spring, when they're hungry from hibernation and the spring berries haven't ripened, or in fall as they fatten up for hibernation. The bears topple garbage cans, rummage through compost piles, and make meals from overflowing birdfeeders. When the bears become too much of a nuisance or get too close to people for comfort, Washington State Fish and Wildlife agents are called. The officers use jelly doughnuts to lure the bears into traps, then transport the animals into the mountains. A specially trained Karelian bear dog drives the beast deep into the wilderness after it's released.

For many years, though, a young boy from the south end, Colton Harris-Moore, proved more problematic than bears or other prowling wildlife.

Like the bears, Colton roamed through backyards. At first, the boy was just sniffing out a meal, hunting for survival. But Colton's appetite grew and he wasn't satisfied with digging through the garbage. He wanted more. He went through neighbors' freezers to find a frozen pizza or chicken fingers, any meal he could heat up, victims said. Then he went through their drawers to find electronics he could steal. He went through their wallets and their computers hunting for credit card numbers and ATM cards he could pilfer. He took their cars, their jewelry, their identities, and their boats.

"It is not just the money value of the items he stole, but the undermining of trust and disturbance of his neighbors; the invasion of their private space," one couple wrote in a March 2009 letter tucked into Colton's thick collection of court records. "Harm was done to people even though he left no physical marks to show it."

CHAPTER TWO

Colton's story begins on Camano Island. He grew up at 925 Haven Place in a modified trailer home with an alcoholic mom, three different father figures and few chances to succeed.

Colton entered into a troubled home life. He was born by cesarean section on March 22, 1991. He was a healthy baby; he and his mom were home within days. There's little public information about the boy's earliest years. Colton displayed unusual behavior as a toddler, hitting his head against the wall. Otherwise, Colton reached normal childhood milestones right on time, his mom said.

By the time Colton was in preschool, his teachers noticed the little boy wasn't keeping up with other kids his age. At three, he qualified for special services. Officials categorized Colton as "developmentally delayed," because he was having trouble speaking the right words. Colton was sent to a special preschool where he got help with speech and articulation. Little Colton was placed on an IEP, or Individual Education Plan, a curriculum specially designed with the help of school counselors and a parent. Colton stayed on his IEP until he turned six and no longer qualified.

Even though the family had been monitored for years by the state, public records do not conclusively identify Colton's birth father. The man likely is Gordon "Gordy" Moore, his family name making up half of Colton's hyphenated surname. The other half was taken from his mother's side. Although court records are ambiguous on the paternal link, a Washington State Department of Corrections photo of the older Mr. Moore shows a striking resemblance to Colton. Pam Kohler, Colton's mother, said she never married Moore, but she believes he is Colton's father.

A drug addict with a history of violence, Gordon Moore was "in and out" of Colton's life during the child's first four years, according to court records. By the time Colton was five, "his father was gone and then in prison for the next several years," a psychologist wrote in a report.

When Gordon Moore visited with his son on Camano Island the get-togethers often turned violent. In May 2003, six months before Colton went on a Thanksgiving vandalism spree, police were called because Colton's dad had gone on the attack. Gordon Moore, then in his mid-thirties, had tossed the twelve-year-old boy into thorny nettles in the backyard. Moore was accused of grabbing the lanky teen by the throat. "Don't you know," Gordon Moore reportedly yelled at his son, "I've killed three men because of my anger!"

Moore's murder claim could not be verified and there is no record that to date he has been charged with homicide. The cops came and took Moore away. "What are you going to do now?" Pam Kohler, Colton's mother, demanded of her son. "They have taken your father away." She reportedly was so drunk she was barely able to stand up.

A short time later, Colton told a school counselor what happened when his father came to visit and threw him into the bushes. The exchange is recounted in court records. The counselor asked if everything was okay with Colton after noticing bruises around the boy's throat. Colton told officials his version of the story.

Colton said he was the one who sounded the alarm when the violent confrontation was out of hand. The boy picked up a phone and dialed 911. After the cops arrived, his mom lost control and began yelling at the police to go away. In a move that later would resonate from one generation to the next, Gordon Moore ran into the woods and hid. Unlike Colton, though, the older Moore didn't get far. The cops quickly caught the man. The school counselor who talked to Colton about the violence at home made a note, "Colton was afraid to go home today."

Gordon Moore worked from time to time as a journeyman concrete finisher. His criminal record includes several arrests for drunken driving. He was sentenced to prison for a hit-and-run-with-injury conviction in 1999 and served prison time, according to records and Department of Correction's officials. Moore's present whereabouts are unknown.

Pam Kohler grew up in Lynnwood, a sprawling suburban area north of Seattle best known now for the Alderwood shopping mall. Kohler said she bought a lot on Camano Island with cash she had saved from working a series of accounting jobs, mostly in Sand Point in Seattle. She told me she worked for the National Park Service until the position was moved to Washington, D.C. "Colt's father didn't want me to go," Kohler said. She took a different position with the National Oceanic and Atmospheric Administration and then a job with the Navy. "It was too hard to commute with a newborn baby and it just was getting overwhelming," she said.

Records show that she paid about $40,000 in 1988 for the five-acre land parcel on Camano Island. (In an apparent snafu, Kohler actually bought the neighbor's lot. The paperwork was sorted out and ownership assigned to the correct lots in 2003.) The dream was to build a home on the lot where the mobile home sits. Today the property is assessed at more than $180,000. The value is in the land. The 608-square-foot mobile home built in 1962 is valued at less than $10,000. Photos on the county's property assessment Web site show a dilapidated building with plastic blue tarps covering holes in the roof and clear plastic covering the windows. The property was transferred in 2007 to Kohler's sister, Sandra Puttmann. Kohler said it was collateral for a loan and the property's title has since been returned to her. The county Web site is slow to post correct information, Kohler said. She still wants to build a new home.

She survives on disability payments because of a broken spine. The injury doesn't hurt much, she said, but it limits her movements. What she hates is that she no longer can split logs. "I love working with wood," she said.

Though Kohler has an antagonistic relationship with law enforcement, she rarely got into trouble that resulted in court dates. There were traffic infractions. For example, in 2005, Kohler was stopped by Everett police for driving without insurance. She was ordered to pay a $538 fine but a judge agreed to lower the fine by more than half, to $250.

When Colton was four, Pam married Bill Kohler. He was a drug addict who was trying to sober up, Pam Kohler told me. Bill Kohler was found dead reportedly of a drug overdose in an out-of-state motel. Colton was ten.

Nearly a decade later, Pam Kohler still doesn't know the details of the death. She never received an autopsy report. "I'm not paying to find out how my husband died," she said. Kohler was helping relatives move from Sedro-Woolley, Washington, to Florida when he died in Oklahoma.

It's difficult to know the influence this man had on Colton's childhood. "He was not really here much," Colton's mom told a social worker. "He was a heroin addict, so he was out a lot. Colton could not count on Mr. Kohler."

Still, there were some intimate moments that sounded like a traditional father-and-son relationship. The two would feed animals on the property. These were cherished, if rare, times.

After Bill Kohler died, another man, Van Jacobsen, moved into the trailer. "Van is not playing with a full deck," Pam Kohler said, according to court documents. The older man sometimes spent time with Colton, hanging out, other times allegedly hurting the boy. State child protective services investigated Jacobsen for abusing Colton, and for using drugs and alcohol, records show. Officials noticed marks on the boy's legs and accused Jacobsen of causing the bruises.

Kohler said Jacobsen isn't a boyfriend, just someone who moved in. "He's not my boyfriend, he never has been," she said. "Colt and I just let him stay here. He just kept kind of coming back."

Colton has a much older half brother, Paul, who for the most part seems out of Colton's life. Paul is more than two decades older than Colton and lives in Granite Falls, a small town at the foot of the Cascade mountain range. He reportedly hasn't been the same since accidentally falling off a three-story roof and suffering a head injury. He had to be rushed by helicopter to a Seattle hospital. Colton told a psychologist in 2007 that Paul hasn't had anything to do with Kohler for years. Colton said he hadn't seen his older brother in more than two years. Unless Colton hung out with his brother while on the lam, he hasn't seen him since he was thirteen.

Kohler disputed Colton's account of her relationship with Paul. She said she rushed to Harborview Medical Center in

Seattle to be at Paul's bedside after his fall. Kohler refused to divulge Paul's last name or who his father is.

The unsettled relationships Colton had with his father, stepfather and mom's boyfriend appear to be tremendous missed opportunities for Colton to form a solid, bonded relationship with a trusted older man. That's a necessary step in a boy's development, experts say. The lack of connection is a common trait in many troubled adolescents, according to Peg Tyre, a Pulitzer Prize–winning journalist and author of *The Trouble with Boys*.

She is familiar with Colton's story by way of national news reports. "He's so extreme and did become a national figure for his asocial behavior," she said.

Whether the relationship with father figures was not available, or those men abused him, or he eschewed the opportunity, the bottom line is that the outcome fit cultural norms for many boys. Young girls are supposed to form close relationships with one another. Their bonds can be celebrated and the close relationships are mirrored on television and elsewhere. Boys are conditioned to become the solitary, stoic archetype of the Marlboro Man, in Tyre's view. Colton appeared to excel in fitting the image. He may not have had a choice.

"Having connection is the most important thing," Tyre said. "It provides the most important psychological boost."

CHAPTER THREE

If the men in Colton's young life were a changing cast, his mother has been a consistent presence, even if her influence has been less than steady. Colton's relationship with Pam Kohler is clearly complex. He continued to turn to her in the most trying of times and in his most desperate moments. Kohler sent Colton mixed messages, at times urging the boy to surrender, at times spurring him on. She delivered her laughable admonishments to Colton via the media, and then begged reporters to print a message saying that he was to call her.

Colton's mother is of average height and a bit heavy (his height must have come from his father's side). Her quick wit and surprising offhand comments—she suggested Colton wear a parachute while flying and scolded him for flying a single-engine plane (only twin engines, in case one fails!)—made her a media sensation. The incongruity of her comments helped propel Colton's myth. Her vocal cords are worn and crusty thanks to years of smoking. Today she favors cheap, generic cigarettes, "filter, nonmenthol," she said. Her face is pocked with gin blossoms, one former neighbor told me. She vowed to shoot reporters who ventured to knock on her door, but sometimes welcomed those who came with cigarettes and beer to trade for a few quotes. She refused to be photographed, but that didn't stop intrepid photographers from snapping her image as she drove down her street in a pickup truck. She has shoulder-length hair that looks as if it has been dyed black.

Kohler and I spoke on the phone dozens, if not hundreds, of times. She never invited me to her home, even though I asked several times. I offered to meet her at a coffee shop or at the newspaper's office, but she refused. Just before one of Colton's court dates in Seattle, Kohler asked me for a ride. She later changed her mind and said she didn't want to attend the hearing after all.

The mother and son reportedly enjoyed a close relationship until Colton was about six, and then it started to crumble. By the time he was ten, "it became clear to him the extent and the damage of his mother's alcoholism," court records say. One time Colton bought her a Bible and an Alcoholics Anonymous book. Kohler burned the AA book.

Colton told officials that she got mean when she drank, breaking the boy's things, yelling and screaming. As Colton reached his teens, she became increasingly violent and angry. She reportedly cared more about her next drink than helping Colton with homework. He told a psychologist that he never got help from his mom on his schoolwork.

By the end of 2005, state investigators had a dozen referrals, and there are more than one hundred and fifty pages of reports on the family. When Colton was four, someone called for help after witnessing Kohler grab Colton by the hair and beat his head severely. Other reports detail times when Kohler told Colton not to come home, and in turn the boy, not surprisingly, didn't want to go home. State officials certainly were aware of the potential for damage in Colton's home. They had flagged at least one incident with a risk factor of "high," meaning there was a good probability that the child abuse would recur. It's clear that the state tried to encourage behavior modification and offered services. It's not clear if Kohler was open to the help.

A former neighbor told me some of the horror stories of living on the same street with the dysfunctional clan. He said UPS packages would be delivered to homes on the street and would disappear. Lawn mowers would go missing and other mischief was common. He said he could hear Kohler screaming at Colton, and he claimed Kohler once told him, "I'm the biggest bitch on Camano Island." The man said Colton was a persistent presence in the neighborhood walking up and down the street with his dog, Melanie. "He would use that dog as an excuse to go onto other people's property," said the man, who didn't want to be identified for fear of retribution.

State social workers tried to get help. One note said, "Mother [said she] is interested in services, but sounds like it will be difficult to get her to participate." The social worker was worried about Colton due to Kohler's drinking. In January 2004, a social worker said, "Mother refuses to get treatment for her drinking."

Social workers made note of Jacobsen's abuse of Colton and the boy told officials Jacobsen twice hurt him. Mom hurt him hundreds of times, he said. She'd go on heavy drinking binges, some lasting two weeks, when she'd break things and go on violent tears. Colton could only try to stay out of the way. He has a scar on his leg from when she threw a coffee mug at him, he reported. In June 2006, a month before his first extended time on the lam, she told him she wished he would die, records show.

"Colton wants mom to stop drinking and smoking, get a job," an official wrote. He wished for food on the table, a full cupboard. Mom refused.

On September 10, 2001, a doctor made a note in Colton's chart: "Assertive, talkative ten-year-old who can become quite angry—but the situation with mother and her boyfriend drinking, living in a tiny trailer, mother drinking all the time, and the physical abuse Colton has gotten from the boyfriend makes his anger easy to understand." Colton told the doctor he was relatively well behaved at school and that the boy was "determined not to get into trouble this year." Colton didn't live up to his hopes.

For Kohler, though, the alcohol was part of the fuel she said she needed to deal with a boy who was growing up quickly and was, at times, way out of control. Colton was shedding baby fat as he grew into his tall frame. He transformed from a kid who probably struggled to get picked by others for school sports to a boy who could have been a prized center on a basketball team. With his height grew his anger and behavior problems.

A doctor noted, "Parent states her drinking helps her deal with Colton and helps her stand up to him." It was a pathetic excuse for her heavy drinking.

Kohler never gave a damn about Colton, one official told me. "He was a nuisance to her," he said.

Mike Rocha is a bounty hunter who for a brief time joined the effort to track down and arrest Colton. He spent hours interviewing Kohler, trying to glean hints about her son's whereabouts. During the talks, he learned about the mother and son's troubled relationship. "He hated that she smoked. He hated that she drank," Rocha said.

The aversion to drugs and alcohol kept Colton sober, for the most part, Rocha said. Probation officers also noted Colton's abstinence from drugs and alcohol. There was evidence that Colton drank beer in the Bahamas, but unlike so many other troubled teens, drugs and booze were not the endgame for Colton. It wasn't because the drugs weren't available on Camano Island or in Stanwood. Although rural and isolated, Stanwood High School still struggled to keep kids off dangerous drugs. In 2010, police and educators held a special forum to discuss a rise in heroin use in the area.

Later, after Colton escaped from a halfway house, he reportedly showed up at a few high school parties near Stanwood and drank beers, probably just as a "social thing," Rocha said.

I asked Rocha why he believed Colton kept returning to his mother, despite the years of abuse and trouble. Rocha said that in his nearly three decades chasing bad guys he had seen even the most hardened criminal return to his mom. It's a soft spot in human nature, an endearment the bounty hunter has taken advantage of to apprehend people.

"Mother's Day is a great day to find people," he said.

When Rocha explained to Kohler how he could help Colton, guiding him through the criminal justice system and seeing that he was held accountable before the law, Kohler didn't seem to care. Rocha said he explained that Colton likely would face police with guns. He told her that her son stood a good chance of being gunned down and killed. I asked Rocha if Kohler seemed moved by his offer and the warning.

"Fuck no," he said. "She didn't give a shit."

CHAPTER FOUR

It's difficult for experts to know the precise origins of Colton's behavior problems.

Dr. Matthew Speltz is an expert in adolescent behavioral problems at Seattle Children's Hospital, a nationally recognized pediatric facility. Like many experts I spoke with, he was careful to point out that it would be unethical for him to speak directly about Colton's case. Still, he agreed to talk because his research and experience are helpful in understanding some of the problems with which Colton likely was grappling.

There's a strain of antisocial behavior that's found among young boys that is fairly persistent and resistant to all modes of therapy, Speltz said. There are a variety of risk factors, some genetic, some environmental. Parenting problems, a difficult home life, and troubles with verbal skills all are risk factors, and Colton's history certainly provides plenty of evidence these were a part of his early life.

The boys Speltz has studied "don't learn to read well and school becomes very unrewarding to them," the doctor said. The inability to read then spirals into all areas of schoolwork and the child often falls behind his peer group, adding to the isolation he's experiencing. Colton was placed in a special school for children with speech and articulation difficulties. The boy also could have attachment issues stemming from poor parenting, especially when he was a toddler. Three different men served as father figures in Colton's life.

Boys who demonstrate serious behavior problems often don't change their pattern until they reach their mid-forties, research shows. Although a small percentage of these high-risk individuals show resilience and can adapt to societal norms, most do not respond well to treatment. "This antisocial trajectory persists," he said.

The child is antisocial, impulsive and temperamental, Speltz said. They often react emotionally, not thinking through what kind of consequences may result from actions. There tends to be a poor control of emotions and an impulsive urge to seek sensations. These kids aren't fearful, the doctor said.

"You can't blame it all on the parents," Speltz said. The doctor said it's a combination of factors, including genes and environment.

Colton's family—his mother and aunt—insist that his disdain for the cops began when police took away a new bike. The story goes that Kohler set money aside and saved up three hundred dollars to buy the bike for Colton's eighth birthday. When the cops saw Colton with a shiny new bicycle, they couldn't believe a penniless kid who lived in a trailer could afford a new set of wheels.

"The policeman put the bike in the trunk of his car and brought Colt home to his mom," Sandy Puttmann, Colton's aunt, wrote to a judge in one of Colton's juvenile cases. "The police asked his mom where Colt got the bran[d] new bike when they were so broke." Colton was "so happy [and] proud of that bike, and then to have that policeman downgrade him and hurt his feelings and accuse him of stealing it," she added. The incident, if true, may help explain Colton's pattern of taunting and fleeing police, which he would repeat time and again.

I asked the Island County Sheriff's Office about the incident. It's a reasonable enough account, detective Ed Wallace said. Colton had developed a reputation as a thief. It wouldn't be the first or last time he was caught stealing fancy toys. The cops might have stopped to ask the boy where the bike came from, Wallace said. It's conceivable a deputy would have grabbed Colton and the bike and whisked him home, to verify the story with his mother. No report would have been written. It just would have been another part of the job.

"Was that the pivotal, traumatic turning point in his life? No, not even close," Wallace said.

As Colton blossomed into adolescence, he spent more and more time with law enforcement, although the relationship mostly was antagonistic. Still, sheriff's deputies and detectives may have filled a void for Colton. By getting into trouble, he found the attention and connection he may have desperately wanted.

"It's such a moving idea," said Peg Tyre, the author who's written about adolescent boys.

Colton wouldn't be the first young man to find that bond with police. Tyre said she's heard from cops who say the kids feel better once they're hooked up in handcuffs. "The kids are happy to be arrested by that guy because they've seen him before," she said.

Delton Young, the psychologist who wrote an eleven-page report on Colton as part of his court files, saw some hope for Colton's future. Young determined that the subject was "not emotionally committed to getting something for nothing."

Colton wasn't driven by financial success or accumulating drugs. Young said Colton needed to develop healthy relationships with friends, teachers, and adults, and needed to achieve success in school and work.

"Colton surely cannot be expected to stay on a positive course living in his mother's home," Young concluded. There was an alternative.

CHAPTER FIVE

Kohler's sister, Sandra Puttmann, had a good relationship with Colton. Both Colton and Kohler described the bond as strong, but it fell apart when Colton was four or five because "some breach opened between Sandy and Ms. Kohler," a report said. Colton had no contact with Puttmann again until he was about fifteen, and by then he was well established on the path to problems.

Puttmann handwrote a five-page letter to the court in 2007. "I love that boy like one of my own," she said. Colton "has come to know my husband and I and respects us," Puttmann wrote. "When he gets out of jail we have offered him a home with us."

"Aunt Sandy reportedly runs a very different kind of house, with appropriate rules and limits needed by young people," Young, the psychologist, wrote in an evaluation of Colton.

The psychologist, hired by Colton's defense team in 2007, didn't acknowledge and perhaps didn't know that Puttmann had written the letter to the judge. In the letter, she displaced blame far and wide for Colton's behavior. Colton got "mixed up in the wrong crowd," Puttmann said. He was a victim of police mistreatment and teachers who used harsh punishments. A school system should help kids succeed, Puttmann said, not degrade them.

After Colton was arrested in the Bahamas, his first call was to Puttmann. When I called her to ask about Colton, she told me almost verbatim what she had told the judge two years earlier. Exasperated, she wanted to know why someone didn't take Colton away from Kohler.

Sadly, there aren't many proven methods for rehabilitating boys like Colton, Tyre added.

Colton was "triply damned," the author said. He came from a really rough family, he didn't do well in school, and clearly had impulse issues. "And yet, he's clearly smart," Tyre said.

Colton's story doesn't track the normal development of a teenager, said Barbara Strauch, a science editor at the *New York Times* and author of *The Primal Teen*, a book that tracks the neurological development of children.

"Clearly this guy is way out of the boundaries of 'troubled teenager,'" she said. "Some kids just are impossible. Is this normal adolescence? No, I would say not."

Even at nineteen, Colton's age at the time of his arrest in the Bahamas, his brain likely was still developing. Research shows that young people's brains still are maturing into their mid-twenties.

Adding to Colton's troubles was years of physical and emotional abuse.

"This guy obviously was reaching out for help all along," Strauch said.

CHAPTER SIX

Colton was diagnosed with attention deficit hyperactivity disorder (ADHD), depression and intermittent explosive disorder.

"It wouldn't be uncommon to have several diagnoses," said Speltz, the child behavior specialist. Comorbidity, the presence of multiple conditions, is rampant with childhood psychiatric disorders, largely a result of the limitations of the *DSM*, or *Diagnostic and Statistical Manual of Mental Disorders*. That's one reason why this catalogue of mental health disorders is being revamped to better address childhood problems, Speltz said.

ADHD is fairly common, as is depression, but intermittent explosive disorder is a less frequent, seldom-used category, Speltz said. The diagnosis tends to result from several discrete episodes or tantrums in which a patient fails to control his or her anger.

"One would have to rule out a variety of other conditions that would account for episodic [behavior]," the doctor said. The doctor making the diagnosis would take into account what precipitated the outburst and compare that to the response. Aggression is an underlying quality that patients must exhibit to be diagnosed with intermittent explosive disorder.

Records are full of examples of Colton's wild rampages. He once broke nearly every window in Kohler's trailer. He could be extremely difficult to handle and sometimes would get into physical confrontations with his mother. She would show caseworkers bite marks she blamed on her son. Colton, for his part, would roll up his sleeves and show social workers the scratches he accused Kohler of leaving. In 2004, Colton was having meltdowns daily. At school he often harassed other kids and bullied them. "Colton is being abusive to mom and the house is a mess," a state social worker wrote the following year. "Colton is out of control."

Doctors tried to treat Colton with medication. He was given Prozac, but that only heightened his agitation. Instead, the doctors wrote him a prescription for Strattera, a different kind of antidepressant, which Colton tolerated, and he began to show signs of improvement. His symptoms of depression, aggression and irritation subsided. "For reasons that are not clear," a report said, "the Strattera was not renewed at some point and Colton does not know why. As a result, the one medication that was clearly beneficial was not applied."

CHAPTER SEVEN

While medical science and pharmacology now offer an array of treatments to help patients with ADHD and depression, few advances have produced viable treatment options for the antisocial patient. "It's remained somewhat resistant to the advances we've made in psychiatry and psychology," Speltz said. "Antisocial behavior has been more resistant to the interventions."

Child advocate author and attorney Andrew Vachss shuns the idea that behavior, especially criminal behavior, can be linked to genetics. "There's zero proof that there's a biogenetic code for crime," he said. "The idea that you can be born bad is nuts."

If genetics could indicate criminal disposition, science would eliminate the Ted Bundys and other serial criminals from the lot. The bad gene just doesn't exist, Vachss said.

Environment and upbringing can stack the direction, but ultimately being bad is a choice. "Evil is a decision, it's not a destiny."

Vachss argues the definition of antisocial behavior disorder is so broad that almost any high school prankster could fall into the category. For example, he wouldn't categorize Colton's burglaries and thefts alongside someone like Kip Kinkel. At fifteen, Kinkel shot his parents, then opened fire at Thurston

High School in Springfield, Oregon, killing two and injuring nearly two dozen more. Kinkel, Vachss would argue, is antisocial. Colton is something else.

Colton likely believed he had no place in the world, no matter where he looked. Then he decided he had to make his own way. That's particularly understandable in today's times, Vachss says. Today, the virtual world blends with the physical. People go online and convince themselves that if their Facebook friend counter reaches five hundred they actually have five hundred friends. "People are not making actual connections with other humans, they're making connections with avatars and icons," Vachss said. "We've become far more detached at the same time we're becoming cyber connected."

Each one of Colton's burglaries and thefts was akin to his Tweets, his Facebook postings, his blogs, Vachss said.

Bev Davis, a neighbor who tried to help Colton, disagrees with Vachss' assessment. Contrary to what some people believe, Colton didn't want any publicity. "He's extremely shy in that way," she said. While some of his behavior would lead people to think he was seeking attention, Davis believes Colton was just pulling a childish prank.

"I can picture him giggling," she said.

Chromosomal disorders are a possible exception to Andrew Vachss' dismissal of a genetic disposition to bad behavior. For example, Klinefelter syndrome is a disorder in which boys are born with an extra X chromosome, XXY instead of the typical XY. The typical Klinefelter patient is characterized as tall, boyish, showing behavior problems, and having underdeveloped genitals. Court records don't indicate that Colton ever received this type of diagnosis. Even if he did, it wouldn't be an excuse for his behavior, but it may help explain some of his actions.

The evaluation of Colton completed in 2007 concluded that Colton "is not a typical antisocial youth." He rarely was violent, didn't have an interest in drugs or alcohol, didn't blame others for his behavior, and didn't appear "glib or superficial." And yet, he seemed to have an unstoppable urge to steal.

PART TWO
MISCHIEF

CHAPTER EIGHT

While most people were stuffing turkeys, baking pumpkin pies and enjoying time with family, Colton was making trouble. He probably didn't have much of a plan that Thanksgiving Day, 2003. He left the trailer where he lived with his mom and Van Jacobsen. From there he probably caught a bus north and off Camano Island.

Like other kids on the island, he often relied on the bus to make the twelve-mile trip to Stanwood. He was much too young for a driver's license. Colton was twelve.

Once he left Camano Island, Colton met up with schoolmates Holden Janssen, Skylar Pennamen and Anthony "AJ" Posey in the small city of Stanwood. There is no town center on Camano Island. Most people from Camano shop at the island's small markets for necessities. When the grocery list gets too long, or they need to shop for clothes or other goods, or if they want to go to the movies, islanders make the trip to Stanwood, a city with a population of about 5,500 residents. In Stanwood, there are bigger grocery stores, fast-food restaurants, a movie theater and the middle and high schools for the Stanwood-Camano School District.

The boys likely started the day at United Mortgage. They pried the door open, snuck in and snatched a laptop. Before they left, they tried to set fire to a window. Later, the owner of the business told the cops he was out $574 in stolen and damaged property.

Then the gang walked about three hundred feet east to the school they attended, the Stanwood Middle School. They broke through a door and went to the gym. Thirsty, they tried to steal soda pop from a vending machine. Frustrated, they instead set fire to the plastic front of the machine. Before they left school, they again tried to light a window on fire. Maintenance workers tallied the damage at $711.

From there, the boys wandered over to the Stanwood-Camano Transportation bus barn and set fire to several recently planted trees. It would cost $220 to replace the trees. Finally, the boys set fire to a sixty-dollar cork bulletin board at the local Thriftway, a grocery store.

AJ was the one who confessed to the crimes, court records show. The day after the mischief, AJ and his father went to the police. AJ told the cops about the three other boys who were in on the mischief, including a Camano Island boy the police already knew well, Colton Harris-Moore.

During the investigation, the boys blundered and pointed fingers at each other. Holden initially refused to cooperate. AJ would deny breaking into the school and Skylar only admitted to serving as a lookout during the United Mortgage burglary. Skylar admitted he set the bulletin board ablaze and tore up the trees, but he blamed another boy for the school vandalism. Skylar said it was Colton Harris-Moore who used a hammer to break out a window at the school. He said it was Colton and AJ who went inside and vandalized the pop machine.

Colton told his story in a written statement. He said he tried to break the door at United Mortgage but couldn't get it to budge. Colton blamed AJ for using a hammer to open the door. Like his accomplice Skylar, Colton admitted breaking into the school; he denied going inside. And he did confess to starting the Thriftway fire and yanking out the trees.

It took a while to sort out the incident. The day's events seem to have been planned by Colton and Holden. The boys told the police that Colton used a butane torch lighter to burn the plastic doorframe at the mortgage office. Then he aimed the lighter at the window until the glass shattered, allowing the boys to scamper inside.

The Stanwood police later crossed the Mark Clark Bridge and drove to Camano Island's south end to pay Colton a visit. His mom, Pam Kohler, let the detectives inside her mobile home, believing Colton was in his room. But when the cops went back to talk with Colton, the door was closed and secured with a padlock. Kohler didn't have a key, but she said she could get in easily enough. In what must have been an alarming sight for the police, Kohler grabbed a hatchet and broke down the door.

Investigators were looking for the laptop that was stolen on Thanksgiving Day. They didn't find the computer inside Colton's room, but they did find a cache of other suspicious items. There was a Sony camcorder, a box of keys and a wallet with someone else's identification. Kohler told the cops she, too, was suspicious of the camcorder, but Colton had told her he bought it at a liquidation store. Kohler told the cops she called Colton's bluff and contacted the store directly. The store couldn't verify the sale. Still, there's no mention that Kohler tried to find out where the camera came from or to take it away from her boy. She did, however, allow the police to confiscate the property found in Colton's room, including the camera.

The incident was just the latest to land Colton in serious trouble. As a seventh-grader, he was suspended from school and later expelled. After being ordered to stay away from the school,

Colton stopped by anyway to visit friends. When school officials confronted him, Colton told them he'd "forgotten" about the no-contact order.

Colton's first arrest was on March 6, 2002, for second-degree burglary. He was ten, a kid with a fuzzy hairdo who was shedding baby fat as he began to sprout into his growing frame. Within a bit more than a year, he'd already racked up seven criminal cases.

Colton's probation officer in 2004 believed he was taking advantage of the system and being opportunistic. Colton presented himself as well behaved and remorseful in the courtroom, but the probation officer feared it was a put-on. The officer wrote, "Colton needs community supervision to address his criminogenic issues and to learn how his behavior affects himself and the community." In other words, he needed a grown-up to pay attention and to create some structure to fully appreciate the damage he was doing to himself and others.

The problem was that the one adult in Colton's life was Kohler. The probation officer noted that Colton and Kohler offered "limited insight on how to avoid engaging in aggressive behaviors at home." The officer recommended both be enrolled in anger management classes and family therapy. The recommendation fell on deaf ears.

If Thanksgiving hadn't gone well for Colton, New Year's Eve didn't go any better. Kohler called the cops after Colton attacked her. Colton was charged with fourth-degree assault.

CHAPTER NINE

Victoria Emerson looked around her classroom at Stanwood Middle School and noticed something was missing. It was March 16, 2004. The digital video camera she kept for special assignments wasn't where it was supposed to be. The next day Nathan Christensen, also a teacher at the school, noticed a handheld walkie-talkie radio was gone. The teachers turned to their students to find out what happened.

Five boys stepped forward with information. Each boy implicated his classmate Colton Harris-Moore. Colton allegedly grabbed both the radio and camera and hid them under his shirt.

Michael Mack, the principal at the school, confronted Colton. Colton explained he couldn't stop stealing and he didn't know why. Colton had already been in serious trouble with the school. He'd been suspended before.

Several phone calls were made. Colton called his mom. The school principal and the school vice principal both called Colton's mom. Finally, Kohler admitted that the school's radio and camera were in her home. She agreed to return the more than seven hundred dollars' worth of property. The case went through the courts and Colton pleaded guilty.

Although six years have passed, Peter Domoto clearly remembers the story of his stolen Zodiac.

It goes like this: Friends were visiting from California and Domoto wanted to show off his little piece of paradise on Utsalady Point along the northern shore of Camano Island. He walked them down the one hundred and fifty steps to his dock.

Before the group reached the bottom landing, Domoto saw a young boy with a dog in a small boat. The boy looked startled. He avoided eye contact with the adults and took off. Only later did Domoto realize the boy likely was trying to steal his Zodiac, a high-quality inflatable dinghy.

The next morning, Domoto woke up with a bad feeling. He immediately went down the long flight of stairs to the water to check on the dinghy. "It was gone," the retiree said. "I figured, well, that's the last I'll ever see of that Zodiac." Domoto filed a theft report.

A few days later, he got a call from a deputy. The sheriff's office had recovered Domoto's boat. A neighbor had called police when she saw Colton stealing an outboard engine, Domoto said. It was a bright, sunny day and Colton couldn't see the woman thanks to a glare on her windows. Four months after the incident at school, the police caught Colton red-handed.

Domoto went down the street to fetch his boat and talked to the deputy. The same boy he'd seen a few days before off his dock was locked up in the back of a patrol car. "Here's Colton sitting in the back of the cruiser with his dog," Domoto remembered.

At the time Domoto didn't know Colton's story. But he remembered asking the deputy if he'd dealt with the boy before. "Do you know this kid?" Domoto asked. The deputy replied, "Oh yeah, we know him."

Domoto said he soon learned that Colton had earned a reputation on the south end of the island. Sure enough, friends from Camano Island's south end told Domoto the story of the boy who broke into their homes looking for food.

"Frankly, I was afraid for him, because even in 2007, and earlier, there were several meetings that the sheriff had on the island mainly to calm people down a little," Domoto said. It's not unusual for neighbors to keep firearms. "My concern was that he would be at the wrong place at the wrong time and someone would blow his head off."

Colton's court-appointed attorney, Staci R. Gossett, argued in court papers filed in the theft case that the boy wasn't guilty of stealing the Zodiac or the outboard motor. Kohler would testify that Colton was home the night the Zodiac went missing, and Colton denied stealing the engine, the attorney argued.

On February 5, 2005, the case went to trial in front of Judge Alan R. Hancock. Colton took the stand in his own defense for about an hour and twenty minutes. Before lunchtime, the judge made his decision. Colton was guilty of third-degree theft. He was sentenced to serve fifty days.

Colton was given multiple opportunities to complete the sentence through community service and other avenues, rather than do jail time. Each time, he blew it. A year after the trial, the judge ordered Colton back to Island County's juvenile jail for fifteen days. The case remained open after his arrest in the Bahamas. There's an unpaid restitution order for $210 for court and legal fees.

Maxine Kostelyk's home isn't far from the trailer where Colton grew up. Reached months after Colton's arrest in the Bahamas, Kostelyk said Colton broke into her garage several times. Only once did he cause any damage.

"He'd take food out of the freezer," she said. Frozen pizza, ice cream and cookies. "He's been [here] a number of times."

She was relieved his crime spree was over and that it ended without physical injuries. Now she hopes Colton gets the help he needs.

"He was just trying to survive, but I also felt that he was very intelligent," Kostelyk said.

Since Colton gained notoriety, she's noticed a change on Camano Island. Now she keeps her doors locked. Her neighbors are vigilant and keep an eye on their property. Colton changed them. Before Colton, this was a peaceful place where homes were unlocked, windows open.

Since Colton's arrest in the Bahamas, people on Camano Island have relaxed a bit, but they're still securing their homes more tightly than before. "We're a little more lax, but we're still locking the doors," Kostelyk said.

After all, there may be other burglars. Colton may have friends or associates; there may be more thugs that follow his barefoot steps. While Colton may be locked up in Seattle, his mom still lives on the island. I asked Kostelyk what she thought about her neighbor Pam Kohler.

"She's got her own problems," Kostelyk said.

Another time the cops found Colton's blood splattered on a wall near a damaged rhododendron bush outside the Stanwood Library. Detectives believed Colton could have been helping someone else clamber up to a window eight feet off the ground. He could have been kicked in the mouth. Or, more likely, Colton cut himself breaking through the window, and then spit his own blood onto the outside wall. Investigators matched the blood sample to Colton's DNA. He made a mess and stole sixty-one dollars and seventeen cents from the library. Colton was convicted of burglary.

There were footprints in the library on that first day of March 2005, but court reports clearly indicate the suspect was wearing shoes. Colton hadn't yet taken to committing crimes barefoot.

CHAPTER TEN

It was supposed to be pizza night for Colton. The thing was, he was wanted on a warrant that night in June of 2006.

When a pair of Island County sheriff's deputies stopped by Haven Place to try to arrest Colton, they had to devise a plan. They anticipated that Colton would try to run off, as he had in the past. As the deputies were sorting out their options, Colton's dinner arrived.

"It just so happened the pizza guy came then," said Detective Ed Wallace, the sheriff's spokesman. The deputies chatted with the deliveryman and they came up with a ruse.

"Let me borrow your hat and shirt," Deputy Luke Planbeck said. Dressed in the disguise, Planbeck took the pie in hand and went up to the house. He returned with Colton in cuffs.

By then Colton was facing mandatory time with the state's juvenile rehabilitation system. He was enrolled in the Lincoln Alternative High School in Stanwood as a freshman, but his prior history forced him to be put on an independent program. He'd been suspended from the eighth grade for kicking another student and for stealing.

A probation officer succinctly outlined some of Colton's problems in a report to the court. "Colton and his mother live alone," the officer wrote. "She continues to minimize his behavior and make excuses for him."

When Colton learned he likely was going to be sent to reform school, he blew off a court hearing. He also blew off school for two months and stayed with a friend. The court was forced to issue a warrant for his arrest.

"The one positive thing that Colton has going is that he doesn't use drugs or alcohol," the probation officer noted.

Colton spent thirty days locked up at the Denny Juvenile Justice Center in Everett. He was released on July 7, 2006, at 1:45 p.m.

After release, Colton faced a turning point. This was the time when he could have decided to change course. He was in serious trouble and knew it. His options were stark and he didn't like the juvenile system, but he didn't like life at home either. Colton could have swayed officials to allow him to live someplace other than the trailer at 925 Haven Place. Foster care would have been an option, although surely Colton would have heard horror stories from other boys about problematic homes. He may also have heard about homes where troubled boys got attention and love. We don't know.

What we do know is that Colton made a decision after his release that afternoon. He decided not to go back to jail and not to return to life with Kohler. Colton soon began his first extended period running from police and not getting caught. He was about to get famous.

PART THREE
WANTED

CHAPTER ELEVEN

The latest skirmish with the cops began early in the day. Colton took off into the woods when he saw the police cars pull into the driveway at his mom's trailer. He knew he was in trouble, but he wasn't just going to surrender. Colton didn't do that—ever. The teen bolted when he saw police.

This September morning, the deputies wanted to bring him in on a warrant. It had been months since he blew off a court date and since then he'd been busy breaking into homes and collecting stolen property.

He knew the heat was on and he didn't want to go back to jail. He was having too much fun. Plus, while living on the run, he'd been sleeping better and feeling less anxious. He wasn't always sleeping in the woods; in fact, most of the time he was crashing in empty vacation homes. It was easy enough to find out when the houses were vacant. He either kept an eye on the house or he could check on vacation rental Web sites to see when the places were available.

The deputies left, but they weren't done looking for Colton. They came back to Kohler's property later the same day. This time Colton hid in the brush. He watched as they barged into his mom's trailer to clear it and make sure no one was home. He watched as the deputies explored the wooded property, overgrown with blackberry brambles. He watched as they took his dog, Melanie, the beagle mix he loved so much. He watched as they went through his campsite collecting the thousands of dollars' of stolen stuff. They even took the clothes he had in his tent.

Undersheriff Kelly Mauck, a veteran of the island police force, later would compare the gear found in Colton's tent with stolen property reports. Every item matched a report. And Mauck took note that the clothes at the tent site clearly belonged to Colton. No other boy he knew was that tall.

There was another piece of evidence found in the camp, one that showed Colton was determined to learn how to fly a plane. There was a flight training magazine that had been delivered to 925 Haven Place, Kohler's address.

When Kohler arrived home, Colton was long gone. He had left a message for her: "Cops were here. Everythings on lockdown," he wrote. "I'm leaving 4-Wennachi won't be back est. 2 month. I'll contact you." Wenatchee is a small city in the heart of Washington's apple-growing region across the Cascades from Camano Island. Colton had friends there, according to his mom.

Colton also told his mom that the cops had taken Mel, the dog. He wrote, "I'm going to have my affiliates take care of that."

Then he added, "P.S. Cops wanna play hu!? Well its not no lil game. . . . It's war! & tell them that."

CHAPTER TWELVE

One of the "affiliates" Colton referred to in the note he left for his mother likely was his pal Harley Davidson Ironwing. Colton probably began hanging with Harley that fall. Records aren't clear on when the relationship began.

Harley was a couple years older and everyone knew Harley was no good. That's why Colton liked him, Harley said. "Back then I was a troublemaker," Harley told me during a 2009 jail-house interview. "He had to come to me. Everyone knows I'm a criminal."

The two young men—very different in appearance—shared rough backgrounds and a kind of brotherhood. Harley has thick, curly hair and a stocky build, but barely breaks five feet, two inches. Colton towered above him at six-foot-two and growing. He had straight black hair and he liked to wear it almost Army-regulation short. In school, both were known for causing problems. The cops knew both boys well and judges in juvenile court had tried numerous times without success to put each of them on straighter paths.

The two would burglarize so many homes each night that "you would be amazed," Harley said.

In late 2006 Colton and Harley had been hitting expensive and empty vacation homes in the woods near where Colton's mother lived, records show.

A typical night of crime would begin with a phone call from Colton, Harley said. Harley would then hop a bus that would cross the Mark Clark Bridge to Camano Island from either Stanwood or Everett, wherever he was living at the time. They'd meet at a rural bus stop and begin breaking into homes.

Harley said he taught Colton to rifle quickly through drawers for valuables. They took laptop computers, jewelry, toys including remote control boats and helicopters, cell phones, Palm Pilots, iPods, and a Trek mountain bike. Night after night, they prowled through homes, all the while doing it for grins.

"He loves his money like I do," Ironwing said. "He wants the same thing, just to have money, to sit on a pile of cash, to throw it up in the air and have it shower down."

After a night's work, Ironwing said he'd hop an early morning bus for home, his pockets filled with stolen property. Colton would stash his take in a tent that he had set up in the woods near his mom's house.

Harley Davidson Ironwing and Colton made a motley crew. Colton was tall and thin while Harley was solid and squat. Harley said he packs a mean punch. His arms are covered with tattoos. Despite the height difference, as Harley tells the story, Colton looked up to him for life advice and for schooling in the ways of criminals.

I caught up with Harley in the fall of 2009, when Colton's infamy was growing exponentially. Harley recently had been arrested and accused of shoplifting at a local shopping mall. He had skipped out on a work release program. We met in a Snohomish County Jail interview room.

Curious about his unusual name, I asked Harley to explain how he came to be named for a motorcycle. Harley told me his name was one of the changes that came after he was adopted at six. He already went by Harley. His new mother added the middle name after the famous American motorcycle maker, and gave him her last name. "She just thought it would be cool," he said. "It gets annoying at times. It's a unique name."

Harley gave me an interview before he spoke to other media outlets, including *Rolling Stone* and network news shows. Before Harley went on national television, I asked him how he felt about the sudden fame he encountered riding his friend's coattails. He shrugged it off. "I'd prefer not to be on the news," he said.

Like Colton, Harley's criminal history dates back to his early teens. Harley was first busted and convicted at fourteen. His rap sheet includes possession of drug paraphernalia, assault, burglary, possession of stolen property, arson and escape, court records show.

Over time, his reputation grew in his hometown. He was known locally as the "Stanwood Burglar. I'd break into anywhere I could get money," he said. Harley believes his bad-boy image is what drew Colton to him.

Harley's MySpace page in 2007 reveals part of his story. He named his body as his best feature, admitted he'd shoplifted, and advertised that he was 96 percent evil. On the Web page, Harley said he preferred coffee to cappuccino and that he didn't get along with his parents. He said he'd done things he regrets, been in fights, would rather wear boxer shorts than briefs, and, after taking a quiz to determine if he was a "true stoner," determined he rated highest, a "certified pot head."

The two boys spent hours together but Colton rarely spoke about his home life, Harley said. They rapped about stuff, about stealing and burglaries. The pair was joined by a bond, a code among thieves. That's why Harley refused to cooperate with detectives as they hunted his friend. Harley would never be a snitch.

"They think I'm full of shit because I won't tell them anything," Harley said. "They got awfully angry at me."

At the time, Harley told me he believed Colton should give up and surrender. "Colton has ambition. He's smart, and he loves what he's doing." Harley said self-portraits were Colton's calling card, but that he needed to stop taking pictures of himself. At the time of the interview, Colton's face was recognizable thanks to a self-portrait police released. There was scant evidence to support Harley's belief that self-portraits were some kind of signature for Colton.

Several times while I talked to Harley he asked me to pass a message along to Colton. Tell him, "Stay out until help can come to him," he said. I didn't understand what that meant and pushed Harley to explain himself. The charlatan grinned at me and said, "He'll know."

After the story ran, an Edmonds woman wrote a letter to the *Herald*'s editor, "I am absolutely furious that I actually paid subscription dues to a newspaper that allows itself to be a message board from one criminal to another." Most people, including many cops, just shook their heads and saw Harley as a nuisance whose information was unreliable at best.

"He had absolutely no useful information," Snohomish County sheriff's spokeswoman Rebecca Hover said. Ed Wallace, the detective with Island County, watched Harley grow up and dealt with the delinquent over the years. Wallace echoed Hover's sentiment: "I would say that any information he provides would be suspect."

CHAPTER THIRTEEN

Colton at times, inexplicably, went barefoot. Not all the time, but frequently enough. Rumors started to circulate of the fleet-footed shoeless teen with a reputation for running from the cops.

It would be a long time before he would earn the nickname "Barefoot Bandit." Barefoot prints were found near his crime scenes and witnesses reported seeing him running without shoes.

"It's interesting how that's become his tag," San Juan County sheriff Bill Cumming would later say. "He's not always barefoot." In the eight years Colton was suspected of committing crimes on Camano Island, he was almost never barefoot, police said. Later, Colton would be connected to a home burglary near Granite Falls, Washington, where a key piece of clothing was stolen: shoes.

"He's not some kid running around with no shoes on," Island County sheriff's detective Ed Wallace said. "He's got boots and shoes." Even Harley questioned the barefoot story. He said he never saw Colton barefoot and claimed the reports of the "Barefoot Bandit" were made up.

Being barefoot for any extended time in the wilderness, where Colton likely lurked much of the time, would be uncomfortable at best, dangerous at worst, said Andrew Toyota, a climbing instructor and volunteer with Everett Mountain Rescue, a local search-and-rescue outfit. Cold feet could lead to hypothermia.

The woods in the Pacific Northwest are filled with thorny blackberry brambles, sharp rocks and all kinds of debris. Even in the driest months of summer, which are rare in western Washington, the underbrush is damp and someone going barefoot almost certainly would suffer cold, wet feet.

Colton's barefoot reputation grew at a time when going barefoot was gaining popularity in some sports. Several runners were adopting the practice of allowing the foot to meet the ground without the padding of athletic shoes, the way the foot was designed. Chris McDougall is the author of the best-selling *Born to Run*, a book about barefoot running. Nerves on the soles of the foot are very sensitive and help runners achieve optimal form. "The really experienced barefoot guys say it's actually safer" to run without shoes, McDougall said. "If you can't see in the dark, then you can feel your way really effectively."

McDougall likened Colton to American Indians and others with long traditions of being both fleet- and barefooted. "He's actually an heir to noble traditions," McDougall said.

CHAPTER FOURTEEN

The Island County deputies knew Colton was expecting a delivery. Colton had broken into a home, stolen a credit card and used the family's computer to order something online. Court records aren't clear, but it was probably bear-strength pepper spray.

The cops were on to him this time. If they could catch Colton with a pizza delivery, perhaps they could use the package to lure him in and arrest him. It was February 2, 2007, at about 5:45 p.m. when two undercover deputies delivered a decoy U.S. Postal Service package to a gate in the 2600 block of South East Camano Drive. The cops hid in the bushes and waited.

The deputies could make out steps on the gravel driveway near where the package was left. Using a flashlight, the cops lit up Colton's face. Colton had his hair cropped short. He was wearing a dark sweatshirt and baggy jeans, records show.

"Colton, stop. You're under arrest," a deputy shouted. But Colton grabbed the box, hopped a fence and ran into the woods through a horse pasture.

Colton quickly outpaced the deputies, but he dropped the delivery package. Just before 9 p.m., a police dog, called in from off island, finished attempting a track. Colton escaped arrest and the chase was called off.

"Colton Harris-Moore got away," the deputy reported. The

cops picked up the box to use as evidence and asked the prosecutor to file an obstructing charge to the long list of other crimes Colton was accumulating. Obstructing a law enforcement officer carries a maximum penalty of one year behind bars for juvenile offenders.

CHAPTER FIFTEEN

Colton had been on the run for six months by now. Mark Brown, the newly elected sheriff, had had enough. He unleashed a new tactic to bring in the fugitive teenage burglar. Brown turned to the media to spread the word to homeowners on Camano Island that Colton Harris-Moore, a sly and quick teen prowler, was on the loose. Brown hoped that by encouraging people to take preventive measures—locking doors and eliminating crimes of opportunity—he'd put an end to Colton's crime spree.

People on Camano Island used to leave homes and cars unlocked. That was before Colton. "There are a lot of people on the island that are very upset and afraid," Island County sheriff's sergeant Brian Legasse said at the time.

The cops suspected that Colton, then fifteen, was packing a semiautomatic pistol and bear-strength pepper spray. They were investigating him in connection with dozens of break-ins.

Colton was living like a fugitive. He squatted in empty vacation homes, slept in tents in the woods and crashed on people's couches—without their permission.

He took credit cards, cash, food and clothing. Sometimes, they say, he broke in simply to take a shower. The effort to catch Colton had been going on for months, "regularly and vigorously," Legasse said.

Each time they got close, he slipped away. "He's young and he's tall. He's got a good stride," Legasse said.

Patty Arnett worked behind the counter at the Tyee Grocery for a decade. She'd watched as Colton grew into his lanky six-foot-two frame. "As he got bigger, his belligerence grew," she said.

Colton knew the south part of Camano Island well. For years, he'd explored the woods and trails that connect roads, shortcuts that could trim miles off a walk to the store.

As the manhunt grew and as reporters started making their way to Elger Bay at the south end of Camano, islanders started sharing their memories of the boy. Diners at the Elger Bay Cafe remembered Colton. Some used to babysit him, waitress Seva Dawson said. People couldn't believe the crime spree, or that Colton could be responsible. On the rural island, people weren't used to hearing about break-ins and crime. "It's something new to Camano Island . . . people are starting to lock doors," she said. "It's sad. Everybody's comfort zone feels a little invaded."

Not far from the Elger Bay Grocery, David Rodenberger had an encounter with Colton. Rodenberger was working in his office when he heard voices outside. The next thing he knew, Colton was standing in the room dressed in a dark sweatshirt and flannel shirt, "what you might expect from a mountain man," Rodenberger said.

"How can I help you?" Rodenberger remembered asking Colton. But the boy flew off into the night, pulling the door shut behind him. "He's a runner," Rodenberger said. And on Camano Island, "there are so many places to go."

Island County sheriff's officials warned islanders that helping Colton and his accomplice, Harley Davidson Ironwing, could result in criminal charges. Residents were told to stay vigilant, lock doors and call 911 with any information that might lead to an arrest.

"I hope someone turns him in," Legasse said. "They'll be saving his life or someone else's."

Colton's mother defended her son. Kohler was confident Colton was living on Camano Island and that he wasn't the threat portrayed by the sheriff's office.

"No fifteen-year-old kid—I don't care how big and strong you are—can do all those break-ins. That's ridiculous," Kohler said. It wasn't the first time she'd downplayed her son's behavior. In previous court filings a probation officer wrote that Kohler would "minimize his criminal behavior and make excuses for him."

This time, Kohler had a bigger audience. As the police began turning to the media in February 2007, reporters, myself included, called Kohler. She rattled off her version of the relationship she had with Colton. She started sharing a story of what she believed her son was doing. She claimed that while Colton may have gotten into some trouble, he phoned her or sent e-mails every day. Each time she spoke to Colton, she begged him to turn himself in, to give up and serve his time.

Court records confirm the e-mail correspondence. Pam Kohler had discussed with Colton her rather curious plan to buy property on a small island in South America. Whether she had the resources to buy the property or what she planned to do there is unknown.

Around this time, Kohler also established a pattern of telling people that Colton had a benefactor. At the beginning of the media interest, when I first spoke with her, the rich people Kohler talked about were Camano Island residents who were treating him well. "I am glad that somebody is harboring him," she said. "At least he's warm and has a full belly." At least that's what she wanted to believe. Over the next few years, she'd repeat the story of a wealthy friend.

Kohler said she repeatedly directed the cops to where she believed Colton was staying. If only it had been so easy, Island County sheriff's sergeant Brian Legasse told me at the time. "If we knew where Colt was, we would have gone and got him," he said.

CHAPTER SIXTEEN

Once Colton broke into a home, he settled in and helped himself to food, surveyed the belongings, and often sat down in front of a computer to log on to the Internet, records show. He may have been able to outrun the cops through the woods, but in the cyberworld, Colton's attempt to cover his tracks failed.

Island County sheriff's detective Ed Wallace detailed in court records his investigation into Colton's use of a computer at Paul Maritz's home on the south end of Camano. Wallace knew Colton's online handles and e-mail accounts. The detective was able to search deep into the computer's memory and use forensic analysis to extract Colton's online activities.

When Wallace searched the online handle "Harris90210," he found several Web pages and e-mails linked to MySpace and Hotmail linked to Colton. Colton used the account "mellenie010@hotmail.com," an apparent reference to Melanie, his pet dog, the numbers perhaps an attempt to link with the teen drama that uses the zip code 90210 for Beverly Hills. Colton was busy sending messages to his mom and friends and using his accounts to order products with stolen credit cards.

Days before Christmas in 2006, Colton logged on and ordered bear Mace, a super-strong pepper spray made to hit a target up to six feet away. Colton arranged to have it shipped to an address on south Camano Island where he could keep watch for deliveries.

Weeks later, on January 20, he checked into his e-mail accounts again. This time he ordered a software program called Evidence Eraser. The software promises to "allow you to completely remove all traces of questionable activity from your system. Formatting your hard drive or simply overwriting the files isn't going to get rid of the data for good," the software's Web site claims. He checked out the fashionable clothes for sale at Raffaello Network, which boasts that it's the largest fashion store on the Net. A poster from his childhood room showed that Colton cut out logos of famous fashion brands.

On January 27, 2007, he logged on several times. Just after midnight, he ordered more bear-strength pepper spray. He also bought thirty-three dollars' worth of "bump keys," a kind of skeleton key, used to "open locks with ease." He checked his e-mail and MySpace account, freely exchanging messages about his burglary exploits with Harley Davidson Ironwing.

CHAPTER SEVENTEEN

Colton also spent time surfing pornography. It's a detail mentioned twice in court documents. He visited a site called BarelyTwinks.com. Detectives described it as a "gay male pornography site." That's a bit of an understatement. The site offers a raunchy tableau of young-looking men engaged in "bareback" action: anal intercourse without condoms. While so-called previews of sex videos are available for free, the site encourages users to buy a membership ranging from $2.95 for a few days to nearly ninety dollars for an annual subscription.

Colton first attempted to purchase a membership on January 17. He couldn't get the site to accept the credit card number he entered. Ten days later he successfully purchased a membership. Detectives assured me that there was evidence beyond the court papers that BarelyTwinks.com was a site Colton visited repeatedly in several homes.

Drawing conclusions about Colton's sexuality, sexual orientation or sexual development based on this single piece of evidence is impossible. Some experts even called the question prurient, salacious and sensational.

Heather Corinna is an online educator who runs the site Scarleteen.com, an online resource about sexuality for teens. She's also the author of *S.E.X.: The All-You-Need-to-Know Progressive Sexuality Guide to Get You Through High School and Col-*

lege. She's answered hundreds of thousands of questions about sexuality, including pornography, from teens around the world.

Unlike pre-Internet generations who had to seek out pornography, today's teenagers can't help but uncover explicit sexual images online. The encounters with the dark alleys of the Web often happen long before most children would have otherwise sought them out, Corinna said.

We don't know how or why Colton stumbled upon the porn site, but it's "not at all unusual" that a boy at seventeen would choose to look at online porn, Corinna said. Although she was familiar with Colton's story, she, like other experts, was careful to say she could only speak in generalities about his situation as reported by the media. "This is obviously someone who was profoundly neglected," she said.

Teens and adults seek out pornography for a variety of different reasons, Corinna said. "It's fantasy material, it's not reality material." People sometimes look for activities they want to replicate in reality; other times its images of acts they'd never consider reenacting outside of a fantasy. For example, some straight women enjoy looking at pornography aimed at gay men, Corinna said. Or the other way around. "The range of reasons why people look at or enjoy certain kinds of pornography is as diverse as people are diverse."

Colton could have been searching out boys his own age for validation that sexual expression was valid, even appropriate behavior. It's almost impossible to know exactly what people are looking for without asking them directly, Corinna said.

The online pornography viewing does suggest that Colton felt comfortable enough in other people's homes to explore such intimate Web sites. Typically children find safety in their own homes to investigate their bodies, hidden behind closed doors in their bedrooms or bathrooms. Colton found that sense of safety outside his mother's trailer, where her drinking and abuse surrounded him.

"It sounds like abuse and neglect may have been his normal forever," Corinna said. "It rips my heart into little pieces."

Although his online behavior doesn't define Colton as gay, as only he can do that, Corinna said she imagines that a gay identity would be another enormous challenge he'd have to overcome. Juvenile jails, prisons and other harsh all-male environments are notorious for being homophobic.

Or Colton could have been playing a game and had no interest in sexual arousal. It's possible that by looking at the BarelyTwinks.com site, Colton may have been deploying a snarky chess move to add an air of confusion to the investigation, or to further his growing mystique.

Months later, I asked Kohler if she believed Colton was gay. She didn't think so. She also didn't believe he was ready to have relationships with girls. "I'm giving him lectures not to get involved with a girl until he's ready," she said. "He's not ready for a relationship."

Colton's relatives reportedly have complained to the sheriff's office about the court reports that detail Colton's pornography preferences. His relatives suggest the computer's owners visited the pornographic sites, an official told me. But my source confirmed that the homeowner was traveling out of the country and detectives found evidence Colton had visited the BarelyTwinks site on computers in several homes.

CHAPTER EIGHTEEN

Colton figured out that it was hard for police to catch a highly motivated and fast teenager. Camano Island regularly is staffed by only one or two deputies at a given time. It can take forty-five minutes to drive from one end to the other. Roads are narrow, dimly lit and winding.

Reinforcements can take more than an hour to arrive. The Island County Sheriff's Office had no police dog. They could call in a dog to sniff Colton down, but the canine unit could take an hour or longer to arrive. The small department was strapped for the kind of resources bigger cities used to track suspects, including helicopters.

By this time in the hunt, investigators had good reason to believe Colton and Harley were armed. Deputies would have preferred better equipment, but they made do with what they had.

On February 1, 2007, two deputies, Chad Eastwood and Matt Mishler, staked out a home on the south end of Camano. They'd received a tip that Colton might be staying there. Sure enough, around 6:30 p.m., the deputies heard voices. It was Colton and his pal Harley.

The boys had gotten their hands on a police scanner and were monitoring the local frequencies, hoping to be tipped off if the cops were closing in on them. Outside, the cops could hear Colton and Harley planning. They'd snagged a credit card and believed they could milk the card for as much as fifteen thousand dollars, enough to buy "anything you want."

Colton and Harley also talked about being prepared for a confrontation. "Did you bring the bullet?" one of the boys asked. Cops believe it was Colton who said yes, and the deputies heard the distinct sound of a pistol magazine being loaded and seated. The cops later learned that Colton had a .45-caliber Ruger handgun, records say.

Just as Colton told Harley, "The apple juice is for you," the deputies made their move. "Stop, police!" Harley dropped a glass full of juice and it shattered on the kitchen floor. Colton bolted into the woods. For a moment Harley froze, then took off after his friend. By the time reinforcements arrived, Colton and Harley were long gone.

The two deputies must have decided it wasn't worth calling for backup. After all, they weren't trying to arrest violent offenders, just a couple of juvenile burglars. But the boys seemed hunkered down, and if the cops had waited for more help, they may have been able to make arrests. It's easy to second-guess in hindsight. Colton proved he had tremendous motivation to avoid arrest.

Detective Ed Wallace said that at least four times he came within feet of Colton. He was close enough to look the boy in the face and see for certain it was he. It wasn't just that Colton was young, had long legs and could outrun the cops. "He always banked on the fact that we would play by the rules," Wallace said. Police don't shoot burglary suspects in the back.

By now, the small Island County Sheriff's Office had logged more than one hundred hours chasing Colton. They were racking up overtime and frustration. That's part of the reason Sheriff Brown turned up the heat on Colton and made public the story of the boy burglar. In a statement released in early February, Brown spoke directly to the teen.

"You will be caught," Sheriff Brown said. "You are hurting the citizens of our community, and you are unnecessarily putting yourself and others in harm's way."

The break came on a Friday night.

CHAPTER NINETEEN

Something flickering next door caught Juanita Rogers' attention. She noticed lights moving in a shed and thought something wasn't right. It was about 8:15 p.m. on February 9, 2007.

Rogers called her husband, Jeff, and her teenage daughter Kaiti to the window to have a look. There was good reason to be alert. For weeks, the papers and TV newscasts were plastered with news of Colton Harris-Moore, the local teenager who'd been prowling homes in the neighborhood for months.

The family believed what was going on next door wasn't right. The homeowner was away and the house should have been dark. Jeff Rogers called 911.

Deputy William Vaughn was the first to arrive. He called for backup. Moments later Dan Waggoner showed up. The two deputies kept quiet and watched. Someone was moving around inside the home. A headlamp was the telltale evidence it was Colton. The deputies recognized the light from previous encounters with the teen.

Knowing that Colton might run, the two deputies devised a plan to make it seem as if the home was surrounded. They shone their flashlights in a way that made it appear their numbers were greater than just two.

By the time Detective Mark Plumberg arrived, the men

decided it was time to try to bring in Colton. Earlier that day, Plumberg was pulled off other cases and assigned full-time to catching Colton. More than ten policemen surrounded the home. "Colton!" Plumberg shouted. After a pause, Colton shouted back. He told the detective he was on the phone with his mom.

The homeowner's brother arrived and told the deputies the layout of the house. He also mentioned someone, probably Colton, had broken in before.

Meanwhile, Colton stayed on the phone with his mom. "My son called me a while ago and he said he was in a house and that the cops had it surrounded and he wanted me to come down there," Kohler said. The cops allowed her to make the short drive and wait outside.

After more than an hour of negotiations, Colton walked outside and was placed in handcuffs. But before they took him away, the cops allowed the teen to talk to his mom. "It went peaceful," Kohler said.

"We're glad that it's finally come to a conclusion, and that he's safe and that hopefully we can put this behind us," Island County undersheriff Kelly Mauck said the night of the arrest.

The police scene on south Camano Island was a bit surreal. Bright lamps from police cars and the flashing red and blue strobe lights broke through the heavy mist and fog of the winter night.

Kohler spoke with her son as he waited in handcuffs in the back of a patrol car. She said she told him he needed to come home to open his Christmas presents, and answered his questions about his dog, Melanie. "He just loves that dog," she said. (Kohler still has the dog.)

She said Colton had waited for a particular deputy, Luke Planbeck, to arrive. Planbeck was the deputy who had dressed up like a pizza deliveryman and arrested Colton before. Colton trusted Planbeck not to hurt him.

Outside the home, some neighbors watched. Others took the opportunity to do more, Kohler told me the next day. "A few people joined hands and said a prayer for Colt's safety."

Kohler said her son had called a few days earlier and was considering surrender. She believed Colton had reached an end, that he gave himself away in an effort to bring a halt to his running.

"I think Colt did that on purpose so he would be noticed and he would be caught," she said. "He wants to come home."

She hoped that he would get help in prison. "I'm hoping before he's released that somebody will find the right medication for him so he can lead a normal life," she said. "He needs a brain scan."

Twenty minutes before Colton was captured, he read an e-mail from supportive friends. Geof and Bev Davis, neighbors on Camano Island, pleaded with Colton to surrender. They knew the boy was in a desperate situation. "We are writing to let you know that we pray for you daily," they said. The correspondence is filed as evidence in the Island County Courthouse.

When Geof Davis saw television commercials for a boat show or other events he could have invited Colton to go to, he thought of his teenage friend. Bev Davis wrote that she wished she could turn back time and offer help to a younger Colton. "We would have tried to help then. Maybe things could have changed for you."

The e-mail tried to convince Colton that he'd already won the battle with police. Colton had proved that he could evade capture. "Why don't you quit while you're the winner?" the e-mail said.

The Davises pleaded with Colton to turn in a gun, if he had

one, even offering to pay him money for it. The letter tried to impress on Colton that he was living dangerously close to the edge. If police encountered him and he was armed, he likely would die. "You are only fifteen, Colt. That is too young to die," the Davis letter said.

Jail offered a safe, better alternative, the Davises promised: "At least in jail you'll be fed, have a bed and be warm."

Reached on a stormy night in October 2010, Bev Davis was reticent. Still, she agreed to share a few thoughts about the boy she watched grow up.

"He's an amazing kid with some problems that should have been taken care of when he was a lot younger," she said. "He was somehow overlooked."

She's surprised he never acted violently. If she grew up in the same situation, she would have been driven to commit far more violent acts. She believes she would have been incarcerated for life.

"I think it's amazing that he's done no worse than he has," she said.

CHAPTER TWENTY

After the arrest that February night, Sheriff Mark Brown took pride in catching the boy. "He's broken into homes, he's used their computers, he's violated their security and well-being," he said. "It's time to put a stop to it." His deputies stopped Colton that night.

Police had feared Colton might be armed with a pistol and bear-strength pepper spray. A can of the spray was found in the home where Colton was arrested. "I can't tell you how grateful I am to talk about a happy ending to a potentially dangerous situation," Brown said.

Just after Colton's arrest, police in Lake Stevens, a bedroom community on the mainland not far from Camano Island, shot a teenager during a burglary investigation. The violent confrontation was what police feared with Colton.

"It was the kind of situation we were afraid would happen on Camano Island," Detective Ed Wallace said. "We believe we are very fortunate" that Colton, Harley or others weren't hurt.

Fun and games. That's what kids think about taunting the police, officials said. Teenagers can't fully appreciate that police confront criminals daily with weapons that easily kill.

"Some of them don't think of it as dangerous or anyone is going to confront them because they're kids. In a dark room, if you find someone in your home you don't know if they're seventeen or thirty-seven or what they are armed with," Wallace said. "This isn't a game. You could be hurt or killed."

The seventeen-year-old boy police shot that morning survived and soon was taken to a juvenile lockup. The potential for that sort of confrontation was always present during the months that Colton allegedly was breaking into homes on Camano Island, Wallace said. It's a danger that persisted through Colton's years on the run.

On Camano Island, neighbors expressed relief after Colton was nabbed. "We can sleep now without worrying about our children and our homes," resident Veronica McCleary said. "I can sleep without a baseball bat under my pillow."

Juanita Rogers, the woman who alerted the cops to Colton's whereabouts, said her family did nothing heroic. She was just glad the boy was behind bars.

"To me it is good to have caught him, but there is a sad part, too," she said. "He's very young and he just needs a friend, a good friend, to talk to him. He needs somebody to show him love and care."

First Colton had to go to the Island County Juvenile Detention Center in Coupeville. The drive itself would have taken more than an hour. Camano Island is detached from its larger neighbor, Whidbey Island. Together the two islands make up the county. There's no quick way to make it from one island to the other. To get from Camano to Whidbey by car, drivers have the choice of going north over the Deception Pass Bridge or heading south to Mukilteo. That's where they can catch a twenty-minute ferry ride to Clinton, then drive another forty-five minutes north to Coupeville, the county seat.

Detectives made the drive with Colton handcuffed in the

backseat, his tall frame making the ride cramped and uncomfortable for Colton.

Hours after his arrest, a judge ordered the boy held on twenty thousand dollars' bail. He was facing at least a dozen new charges that could keep him locked up for the rest of his teenage years.

"We have the ability to keep him; it is important to us that he not get out," Island County prosecutor Greg Banks said. Prophetic words.

The charges stemmed from the raid on Colton's tent camp in his mother's backyard. Detectives recovered a cache of stolen computers, cell phones, jewelry and pricey remote-controlled toys. Banks couldn't charge Colton as an adult because he didn't commit violent crimes. The longest the prosecutor could lock up Colton was until his twenty-first birthday. "It is safe to say he is looking at a sentence measured in years, not in days," Banks said at the time.

Colton was connected to a "crime wave" on Camano Island that had been "terrifying for folks," Banks said.

Colton appeared a few days later in court wearing a bright orange jumpsuit. When he entered the small courtroom and saw reporters aiming cameras at him, he looked surprised. "Paparazzi," he said.

Special deputy prosecutor Colleen Kenimond asked Judge Alan R. Hancock to increase Colton's bail to thirty-five thousand dollars. She cited Colton's lengthy criminal past and the threat he posed to neighbors. "We're concerned he stay put," she said. The judge was the same one who had convicted Colton in the Zodiac theft two years before. He agreed with prosecutors and increased bail.

A court-appointed defense attorney, Rachel Hintzen Miyoshi, told the judge that Colton didn't have the money to post bail and is "not going anywhere."

I called Kohler to find out if she had money, if she would post bond. "I don't ever bail anybody, I don't care who it is," she said.

With Colton in jail, the police still hadn't captured Colton's accomplice, Harley Davidson Ironwing. In an effort to increase pressure on the older boy, police distributed wanted posters featuring Harley's mug to statewide media.

Later that night, after seeing his image beamed on a television news program, Harley turned himself in. Harley pleaded guilty to the Camano Island crimes and was ordered to serve up to fifty weeks in juvenile detention.

CHAPTER TWENTY-ONE

Back on Camano Island, life settled down and the edge of worry softened. "A sense of calm has now taken over," Elger Bay Grocery manager Deidre Chamberlain said.

Days after the arrest, Sheriff Brown drove back to south Camano Island where he met with about a hundred and fifty people at the South Camano Grange. "A lot of people's privacy was violated, their homes entered, their homes burglarized, their computers used," the sheriff said. "This is a huge impact on the citizens of the island and I want to make sure I treat it properly and address their needs."

The fear of what could have happened was still palpable. People wanted to know how to clean up the mess Colton left behind. On an island where most people kept their homes and vehicles unlocked, now people talked about bolting their doors and keeping their kids inside. One man threatened to shoot anyone who entered his home. The standing-room-only crowd peppered Brown with questions.

Why did it take so long to bring Colton in? Where were the police dogs? What about using an electronic stun gun, or Taser, to snare the elusive teen? Shelby Shondel said he'd urged the cops years ago to use a dog to track the boy. Shondel lived on Haven Place, a neighbor to Kohler and Colton. "Now I'm hearing you tell me this kid could have used an automatic weapon?

This could have been over months ago if you'd used a dog," Shondel scolded.

The small department does not have police dogs, although it had arranged to use dogs as needed from neighboring departments. Budget cuts in 2010 forced Island County to trim resources even more. Any chances of getting a dog now are gone.

Kohler was defiant after the arrest. She was convinced that Colton couldn't be responsible for all the crimes on Camano Island. She expected he would spend more than a year locked up and was making plans for him to live off the island after his release.

Her immediate concern at the time was raising enough money to hire a private attorney. "The best way to help him is to help him get a good lawyer," she said.

It wasn't until Colton became a national celebrity that Kohler tracked down a good attorney. In 2007, as Colton faced nearly two dozen felony crimes, he was represented by a court-appointed attorney.

There was no trial. Prosecutors agreed to a plea deal.

"This conviction and plea agreement serves the purposes of the juvenile justice system," Island County prosecutor Greg Banks said in a statement. "Mr. Harris-Moore will be held accountable for his crimes by a lengthy sentence, even by adult standards."

An Island County Juvenile Court judge sentenced him to at least three years behind bars. Had he served all the time, he would have been nineteen on release.

Under the plea deal, Colton was required to repay all his victims. He was to be held by the state Juvenile Rehabilitation Administration (JRA). The state would give Colton a structured environment, school and counseling. They'd help the kid turn himself around.

He could have gone to trial and faced as many as twenty-three counts. The deal with prosecutors paved the way for Colton to succeed while serving his time in the JRA.

Colton was transferred out of the Island County juvenile detention center to the JRA in July 2007. He first went to Green Hill School in Chehalis, the most secure center in the state for boys. The school tries to help kids learn work skills and provides treatment for a variety of problems, including drug dependence, sex offenses and mental health issues. There's a photo CBS News obtained of Colton towering over Kohler with a Christmas tree behind them. Colton is wearing a GHS sweatshirt and smiling.

While the state keeps each juvenile's file private, Dan Robertson, a spokesman for the JRA, reviewed what he could of Colton's case file with me. In hindsight, state officials called Colton's case atypical.

"Colton was doing very well in an institution," Robertson said. "He was doing very well in high school. He was truly engaged in the treatment program."

Counselors and psychologists evaluate the thinking and behavior of each prisoner. They try to teach the students skills about aggression and social interaction. The goal is to stabilize them emotionally and socially. "We have psychologists, consulting psychiatrists, medical personnel, pediatricians," Robertson said. Colton would have been treated using cognitive behavioral therapy, treatment that reinforces appropriate behaviors.

The state put Colton through a number of assessments and determined he was doing well enough to be moved from Chehalis to Griffin Home, a halfway house in Renton, a suburb south of Seattle. Although the staff at the school was always present and doors were locked, Robertson made it clear that the home wasn't a fenced-in, secure building. "It's not a jail," he said.

At Griffin Home, Colton was taking high school classes and learning vocational skills.

"Work experience is really important for when they leave," Robertson said. The system puts great value in getting kids out of the maximum-security reform schools and into structured environments that feel more like home.

"Minimum security is a really good opportunity for youth to make good decisions," Robertson said.

Colton was brewing a plan. He was trying to decide whether to stay at Griffin Home. He was pissed off because the officials who ran the school wouldn't let him wear sunglasses inside. Colton made his decision.

"Colton made a very bad decision. He ran, he absconded."

Officials wondered—after the escape—if Colton had manipulated the system.

Two days later, a man reportedly saw Colton fishing at Lake Ki near Arlington, more than fifty miles north of Griffin Home.

CHAPTER TWENTY-TWO

About a month before Colton escaped Griffin Home, his former accomplice was back on the streets of Stanwood.

Harley Davidson Ironwing went on a mini–crime spree of his own. He was accused of using his elbow to break a window in a Stanwood flower shop. He broke into the till and took what he could, about a hundred and fifty dollars. Then he went to a nearby hair salon, kicked in the door and took twenty dollars from the cash register, court documents said.

"It was very upsetting," the salon owner told me. She asked that her name not be used, fearing retribution.

Days later, Harley attended a Sunday service at the Cedarhome Baptist Church, also in Stanwood. His mind wasn't on finding God. While the congregation prayed, Harley, then eighteen, snuck down into the basement. A pastor discovered him trying to get into the church safe. The lockbox was filled with thousands of dollars collected from the congregation.

"He left in the middle of the service to steal from church, and that's not cool," Stanwood police detective Tedd Betts said at the time. "There are people at church that if he would reach out to them, they would help him." Instead Harley decided during prayer services to steal from the church.

Harley was arrested, ordered held on forty thousand dollars' bail for investigation of five counts of second-degree burglary and one count of first-degree attempted theft. Harley admitted his crimes, which was welcome news to the salon owner. "Hopefully as a young person, he'll learn and be able to make changes in his life," she said.

The detective had similar sentiments for Harley. It wasn't as if Harley was homeless with no options. He had a place to stay but decided instead to steal to get by, Betts told me. "This isn't a case where his parents died and he's got to survive. He made the choice not to go to school. He made the choice to commit the crimes he did."

Betts said Harley could now choose to turn things around, to access community resources. But the detective was not hopeful. "The statistics show we may be dealing with him again," Betts said. "The ball is in his court."

The detective was right. Harley wasn't through committing crimes.

CHAPTER TWENTY-THREE

Colton escaped. Pam Kohler got the call around 11 p.m. It was a counselor from the group home where Colton had been living. Colton had opened a window and slipped away from Griffin Home. The Barefoot Bandit was gone.

Counselors noticed the empty bed around 9:30 p.m. on April 29, 2008, and sounded the alarm. But it was too late.

Colton had been complaining to his mother that he wasn't getting the necessary medical attention for an eye problem, reportedly something to do with glare from overhead lights. The group home wasn't allowing Colton to wear sunglasses inside. That story didn't jibe with what some of his housemates at the juvenile group home said. The word was that Colton was being a big baby about his eyes; others believed he was just using a ruse to get attention.

Kohler said if her boy showed up on Camano Island or called she'd tell him to give up and surrender. "I hope he turns himself in and gets this over with so he can go on with his life," she said.

Colton never turned himself in.

Just after the escape, I was contacted by a source inside Griffin Home. "Please don't identify me," the source said in an e-mail. The writer explained that the eye problem was bogus, a ploy Colton had cooked up before the escape.

"He has been trying to look 'cool' by wearing dark shades inside buildings and classrooms, which is a violation of the home rules and Renton School District rules," the writer said. It's a rule because teenage drug users sometimes wear shades to conceal blurry eyes brought on after sneaking a high. The writer told me that Colton had been to an ophthalmologist the morning before he escaped. The eye doctor refused to write him a prescription for dark glasses. "Colton was angry about that and had been having attitude [and] behavioral issues for several days," the writer said. It's unclear if Colton was using drugs or just wanted to wear shades inside.

The escape didn't come as a surprise to the people trying to help Colton in the home. "He is a very angry young man who has yet to really accept responsibility for his previous actions; he still brags about outrunning the police for several months," the writer said.

Harley Davidson Ironwing told me he'd been a prisoner at Griffin Home, although not when Colton was there (officials don't allow codefendants to be housed together). Escaping, Harley said, was as easy as opening the door. "They tell you, if you're going to run, go ahead," Harley said. All they can do is call the cops.

News of the escape annoyed the Camano Island community. Sheriff Brown issued a press release. Privately the sheriff pointed out that there was little his department could do but wait to see if Colton would return.

The escape officially fell to the responsibility of the Renton City Police Department. It would be up to prosecutors in King County to file escape charges. To date, no charges have been filed in the case. When adult prisoners escape from the state Department of Corrections, the state has the ability to issue a so-called secretary's warrant. The state DOC has its own police force with the authority to track fugitives or parolees who have violated their terms. No such system is in place for juveniles who flee the system.

This didn't mean Colton wasn't in serious trouble. Back in Island County, Sheriff Brown was upset that the prisoner his department worked so hard to apprehend had slipped out of the system so easily. Not only did Colton skip out on the time he owed to the state; he also blew off the thousands of dollars in restitution he agreed to pay his victims as part of his plea bargain.

It wasn't long before a familiar pattern of break-ins on Camano Island resumed. The problem that the cops had ended with Colton's arrest on February 9, 2007, returned. Colton was back.

PART FOUR

BURGLAR RETURNS

CHAPTER TWENTY-FOUR

The Mabana Fire Station on Camano Island's south end was broken into several times during Colton's crime spree. Shortly after his escape from the halfway house, he took the station's infrared device. It's used by firefighters to quickly assess where people could be trapped inside a burning home or to find someone lost in the woods. The device also works as night vision goggles. Colton added it to his collection of expensive outdoor toys.

The small island fire station wasn't out the expensive piece of equipment for good. They'd get it back later that summer, after the police came close to catching Colton.

The roads were nearly deserted late on the summer night of July 17, 2008. It was more than two months since Colton had escaped Griffin Home. When Island County sheriff's deputy Bill Vaughn spotted the Mercedes, the luxury car was being driven too fast. It was all over the place on the road. As Vaughn pulled behind the car, the driver sped up. A chase was on.

At first, Vaughn didn't know the car was stolen. He didn't realize until later that the driver was Colton Harris-Moore.

Colton must have seen the cop in the rearview mirror and freaked. He hit the gas and took off. Behind the Elger Bay Grocery, Colton slowed down enough to jump out of the moving Mercedes. Like he had so many other times, Colton disappeared into the woods. But before Colton could get away, Lucas Adkins, a reserve deputy riding in the patrol car with Vaughn, got a good look. Adkins recognized Colton. Even so, the deputies had a more urgent public safety issue to handle. The Mercedes continued on with no driver behind the wheel and crashed at slow speed into a propane tank, breaking a pipe.

"An officer turned the propane off," Shirley Morgan wrote in a victim's statement. She owns the café adjacent to the grocery store. "This could have resulted in a much more serious crime if it weren't for the officer being alert enough to turn off the propane."

The car belonged to Carol Star, a neighbor of Pam Kohler's. When the cops reached Star, she was in Colorado. No one, certainly not Colton, had permission to drive her car.

"I'm convinced it was him," Sheriff Mark Brown told me the next day. "He spit in the eye of law enforcement. He spit in the eyes of the juvenile services that tried to help him and he spit in the eye of the citizens that have tried to help him."

The cops tried without success to capture Colton. A police dog from Everett, the closest big city to Camano Island, nearly ninety minutes from Elger Bay, was called in the next morning. Later in the day, a team of heavily armed police from Marysville, a smaller city just north of Everett, crossed the bridge to Camano Island to help out. The Marysville cops had been trained in man tracking. Wearing camouflage uniforms, they scoured the woods and fields for clues. Despite the impressive show of force, no one was arrested.

It all seemed like a flashback to February 2007. Again the sheriff's office was handing out mug shots of Colton; again neighbors were talking about the teenager's exploits.

The stories again circulated that Colton slipped out of his shoes, climbed trees and slept in the woods. Again, victims recounted how he used home computers, stole credit cards and ate people's food.

"Ever since he was a little guy, he's never thought through if he did something, what would happen," his mom told me. "He don't think of the end results. He never has."

Islanders blamed the teenager for changing their way of life, Josh Flickner told me. Flickner is the manager of the Elger Bay Grocery, where Colton crashed Star's Mercedes. "The whole island is tired of putting up with someone who has a blatant disregard for right and wrong," Flickner said.

That day, while reporting about the crashed stolen car, I ran into Kyle Howe and Shay Quick, both seventeen. They grew up with Colton.

He'd always been a problem, they said. He liked to egg people on, throwing rocks at passing cars, looking to be chased. At the time, south Camano Island was the only place Colton knew. The boys said he knew it well. The cops probably couldn't catch him if he slipped away into the dense underbrush. "If it turns into a wood chase, no way, the kid's too fast," Howe said.

Still, Howe believed his former classmate would be caught. "Sooner or later, he's going to do something stupid," he said. This was in July 2008, two years before Colton's run would end.

Camano Island residents voiced their worry about what would happen next. People feared a violent, even deadly confrontation.

"He's a kid who's basically being a dumb kid," neighbor Patrick Campbell said. If Colton kept it up, "he could be a dead kid."

Colton's mom didn't believe Colton took her neighbor's car. But Kohler did have a hunch he was back on Camano Island. As she had said before, Colton was being cared for and was staying with a generous family on the south end of Camano. She didn't know precisely where that home was.

Kohler's sister, Sandy Puttmann, insisted that Kohler called the cops repeatedly telling them where to find Colton, but the police didn't listen. Sheriff's officials scoffed at the story. If they knew where Colton was, they'd arrest him. And if there was a benefactor, that person faced possible criminal charges for rendering assistance. But there was no evidence to corroborate Kohler's claim that Colton was safe with a rich benefactor.

Detective Ed Wallace said police never found evidence that Colton had a secret accomplice or some rich family who was caring for him. "If he had a benefactor, why continue?" If there was someone out there helping Colton, the cops would have found something, or a neighbor, someone would have called the police. To date, even after his arrest in the Bahamas, nothing has been released about an accomplice or benefactor.

Kohler said she pleaded with Colton to bring this scary and senseless chapter in his young life to an end. "I have talked my head off to him about turning himself in, and he said he's working on it," she said. Kohler said she heard from Colton; he called her at home from time to time.

Despite her pleading, she doubted he'd give up soon. It was the middle of the Pacific Northwest summer. The weather was glorious, the days long. "I really don't think he'll do it in the summertime. Who wants to leave the good weather and go to jail?"

CHAPTER TWENTY-FIVE

The best criminals don't leave evidence for the cops. No fingerprints or stolen property. Nothing that can pin a suspect to a burglary or assault. The experienced bad guys know to wear gloves, hide their faces and clean up good and well. Colton hadn't quite figured this out. He almost always left evidence behind.

Carol Star's Mercedes held a treasure trove of evidence. When Colton bolted, he left behind a SwissGear backpack, also stolen from Star, full of stuff.

"He's not some criminal mastermind," Island County sheriff's detective Ed Wallace said. "A criminal mastermind doesn't leave us this."

Along with the backpack, the cops found the infrared device that had been stolen the week before from the fire station on Camano Island.

It was what Colton stashed in the backpack that opened up Colton's world to investigators.

There was a journal with Colton's name written across the front. It contained handwritten lists of credit card numbers that matched those of Camano Island residents whose identities had been stolen. The journal had some notes and plans, but it didn't contain Colton's innermost thoughts, deep revelations or secret desires.

The cops found a wallet filled with credit cards belonging to Michael Nestor. Days earlier Nestor had contacted police to report that his vehicle had been broken into and credit cards and other important personal documents were taken.

A Magellan Maestro, a portable global positioning system, was found. Theodore Lavigne reported the electronic device stolen on July 19, two days after the car chase.

There were two magnetic credit card readers in the backpack, too.

Colton ordered these card-reading devices using a stolen credit card that belonged to Jim Pettyjohn, a grandfather and retiree who lives with his wife of more than forty years, Carolyn. The Pettyjohns' home is about a mile south of Kohler's trailer. The couple weren't certain, but they believed that Colton, as a younger child, likely spent time with other neighborhood kids in their yard, on the trampoline. Like other children in the area, Colton probably helped himself to Cokes and Popsicles from their well-stocked refrigerator and freezer.

"It was just a fun place," Carolyn Pettyjohn said. Jim Pettyjohn explained how they raised three girls in the home and now regularly entertained grandchildren. "Our home has always been a headquarters for the kids," he said.

Back home, "you never even took the keys out of the cars at night," he said, his accent giving away his Texas roots. Society has changed in seven decades, he admits, but Colton hastened the loss of safety in the Pettyjohn home.

The Pettyjohns weren't expecting trouble, but trouble, by way of Colton, found them. The couple first noticed something wasn't quite right with their credit cards when an item showed up on a statement from an out-of-state sporting goods store. After a phone call to American Express, the charge was reversed.

"They gave us credit for it and we didn't think anything about it," Jim Pettyjohn said.

Later, Jim Pettyjohn ordered a book online. When a FedEx delivery came, he just assumed the package was what he was expecting. He opened the box and discovered two small electronic devices and a compact disc. Frustrated, he believed he'd mistakenly ordered an electronic version of the book. He set aside the box and package for the weekend, when his tech-savvy grandson could help him load the book on his computer.

When the weekend came, the package was gone. They looked high and low, checked the garbage cans, but there was no sign of it. "The next thing to happen was when the police guy called us—'Mr. Pettyjohn, are you aware that Colton Harris-Moore has all your credit cards?' "

Pettyjohn reviewed his recent credit card statement and found several unauthorized charges. One was a $469 bill from ScanCity, the company who sent the credit card readers. There also were ten purchases at iTunes, an online music store, totaling $485.44. Songs on iTunes cost about ninety-nine cents each, so Colton managed to quickly load an iPod with nearly five hundred songs. (Police reports don't say what Colton's taste in music was.) A charge to PayPal, an online bank, came to more than three hundred dollars.

Police believe that Colton had staked out the Pettyjohn home. First, he snuck in quietly at night to slip the credit cards out of Pettyjohn's billfold. Colton carefully took out four bank cards, copied the numbers into his journal, including the three-digit security codes, and then put them back precisely where Mr. Pettyjohn kept them. Pettyjohn said he didn't notice that someone else had been through his wallet. The second time Colton came back to retrieve his FedEx delivery.

"He's very clever," Carolyn Pettyjohn said.

Colton also managed to slip in and out of the Pettyjohns' home without disturbing their two dogs, a dachshund and a "yappy poodle." "They bark at anybody," Carolyn Pettyjohn said. They hadn't barked when Colton twice slipped into the office.

In hindsight, the Pettyjohns said they don't think much about the whole incident. It was "no fun" to sort through the credit cards and have them replaced, but that's just the way it goes, they said. "Things are going to happen to you," Jim Pettyjohn said.

You can't help but feel for Colton, he said. "You kind of say, 'Bless his heart,'" he said. Still, Jim Pettyjohn said a young man like Colton would have met the strong end of a baseball bat where he came from in Texas. The boy would have gotten a "whopping."

"Everybody hates a thief, but in a way you can understand," Carolyn Pettyjohn said.

The two devices Jim Pettyjohn pulled out of the FedEx box, the ones that Colton stole and later were found in the backpack, are designed to pull data off credit cards. Detective Ed Wallace showed me a page in one of the three huge binders that hold evidence in Island County's ongoing investigations on the Barefoot Bandit. He showed me a printout of the information he was able to retrieve from the devices. It was lists of credit card numbers and other personal information. Colton would have had to "dial for dollars" with the information. Not all of what he swiped gave him enough information to make purchases. He had to, through trial and error, go through each number to test the accounts. Then, once he found an account he could draw against, he'd have to spend with urgency.

"If you're going to use a credit card, you're going to burn

them up quick," Wallace said. Colton likely knew he had limited time to use the stolen identities.

Detectives found two cell phones in the backpack that had been used to dial Pam Kohler's number and Green Hill School, the juvenile detention center in Chehalis where Colton had been locked up. Colton had programmed the school's number into the phone and called there twenty-one times. When an Island County detective checked with officials at the school, they confirmed several hang-up calls. It appeared Colton was trying to reach one of his former schoolmates.

A digital camera and two digital memory cards with dozens of photos stored on them also were among the evidence. The pictures had been deleted, but Wallace was able to access the images. They were all snapped on or around July 8, 2008. Colton had snapped sixty-eight pictures of himself. Some show Colton smirking, others looking away. Most of the images appear to be taken in the same place, all with Colton holding the camera at arm's length and peering back into its lens. Sheriff Mark Brown asked the detective to choose the best photo and release the image to the media. Colton created his own wanted poster.

The image, now iconic and splattered across magazine spreads and television news broadcasts, shows a smirking Colton. He's on his back in the woods wearing a Mercedes logo polo shirt, listening to an iPod, and surrounded by junk food and an emergency flashlight.

"Catching Colton Harris-Moore and putting a stop to his criminal activity is currently the top priority for your sheriff's office," Brown told Island County residents.

The backpack also held a small mirror with the unique patterns of Colton's fingerprints. Mirrors were a common item found in Colton's camps. He must have filled his time peering into his reflection—looking for what? Did he find comfort in the boy's face he saw? Was he looking for signs of growing up? Did the reflection hold some answers for him? Or was he simply obsessed with his eyebrows, his grin, his bangs, eyes and mouth? Did he giggle as he watched the mirror, as he stuck out his tongue or made faces?

Wallace believes Colton was in love with Colton.

"He's a little narcissistic," Wallace said. "He likes to look at himself."

CHAPTER TWENTY-SIX

Most of the time Colton targeted homes and businesses. Sometimes he created places where none existed before, including the address 550 Haven Place.

Colton grew up at 925 Haven Place. It's a rural street and the mailboxes for the block are nailed to a two-by-four in one central location, saving delivery time. At some point, someone added a mailbox to take delivery for the address 550 Haven Place. There is no 500 block on the short country road.

"550 Haven Place does not exist," Detective Mark Plumberg wrote in a report. "The mailbox just appeared on the road among other mailboxes since the escape of Colton Harris-Moore."

The mail started coming. Lori and Ronald Free's home was burglarized on June 23, 2008. The couple was away on a fishing trip. When they returned, they learned that someone was applying for credit cards under Mr. Free's name. Chase Bank issued a card and mailed it to the 550 Haven Place address.

Further investigation led Plumberg from the mysterious mailbox to an automated teller machine at the Whidbey Island Bank branch on Camano Island. There were several suspicious withdrawals and withdrawal attempts made with a stolen card. ATM machines are monitored with secure video surveillance. Plumberg checked the videotapes recorded at the time of the withdrawals. "Colton Harris-Moore can be seen on camera at the ATM manipulating the machine," Plumberg noted. The videos were entered into evidence.

All from an address that doesn't even exist.

Colton made it off Camano and wandered north to the San Juan Islands. More remote than Camano, the San Juans are accessible only by boat or plane. Seawater temperatures remain around 48 degrees Fahrenheit, too cold to swim long distances. The Washington State Ferry system serves four islands in the archipelago, Lopez, Shaw, Orcas and San Juan. These are popular tourist spots, especially in the summer. Remote, pristine and gorgeous, the islands offer a quiet getaway. The few small towns in the San Juans are filled with bakeries, gourmet restaurants and pottery shops. High-speed boats offer rides to catch glimpses of the region's resident orcas, the black-and-white mammals better known as killer whales.

Although some locals gripe about the summer visitors, the tourist business fuels the island economy, providing a financial layer of fat to survive the damp, cold winters.

One hundred and seventy pieces of land rise out of the water to constitute islands in the San Juan archipelago. Add in reefs, rocks and other small clumps of soil, and the number rises to more than four hundred. When the tide is low, the count jumps to almost 750.

Although the islands appear small on a map, their combined footprint fills hundreds of square miles. Orcas and San Juan islands are almost identical in size, both about fifty-five square miles. If San Juan Island is shaped a bit like a pear, Orcas is more like a balloon that's been squeezed at the middle, the bulk of the landmass collected at two ends.

Like many vacation spots, the population drops precipitously in the winter months. Homes sit vacant, save for a few storm watchers and the sparse group of locals who make these islands their year-round home.

During at least two visits to the San Juan Islands, Colton allegedly committed as many as thirty burglaries, Sheriff Bill Cumming said.

Police suspect Colton was connected to burglaries at the Deer Harbor Marina, on the westernmost flank of Orcas Island. He prowled through the town of Eastsound, the few blocks that contain the island's small commercial district. The roster of businesses he hit reads like roll call at a local chamber of commerce meeting. He allegedly broke into the Sunflower Café, a bakery; Vern's Bayside, a tavern and restaurant; Bilbo's Festivo, a Mexican restaurant; Islanders Bank; Ace Hardware; the Island Market; and Homegrown Market.

His burglaries became a quotidian occurrence.

Sharon Mudd got to work in the predawn dark on September 8, 2009. It was 5 a.m. when she flipped on the lights inside the Island Market, the largest grocery store in Eastsound, the biggest town on Orcas Island. Mudd immediately called the cops and her boss, Jason Linnes. Someone had broken in overnight. The place was a mess. The small automated teller machine was knocked over, water was everywhere and the distinct smell of bleach clung to the air.

The store owners have declined media interviews. An affidavit filed in San Juan Superior Court provides details of what investigators believe happened.

The cap from the bleach container was in one of the supermarket aisles. It looked like someone tried to use the bleach to erase any evidence from the broken ATM machine. Whoever broke in likely forced open a door and pried his way into several offices.

The intruder was captured on video surveillance. A tan, thin, youthful man could be seen prowling the store. He raised an arm over his face, trying to avoid the prying eyes of the surveillance video.

The camera only caught glimpses of the burglar. In one shot, he's moving a pallet jack, a hand truck designed to move heavy loads of groceries. Another image shows him moving toward the store's kitchen, a shirt wrapped around his left hand.

Colton must have cut himself while trying to break into the small cash machine at the front of the store. There was blood on the sink, enough for detectives to collect a sample and have the evidence tested. They wanted to see if it matched any other DNA samples in the state's database of felons. The match came back as Colton Harris-Moore. When the state's lab completes a DNA test and determines a match, the chances it could be wrong are one in 150 quadrillion.

Detectives from San Juan County forwarded the videotape to Island County. The Island County deputies confirmed that the person in the Island Market was Colton.

The evidence was used to file a criminal complaint charging Colton with one count of second-degree burglary. Bail was set at twenty thousand dollars, but no one expected Colton to make his date.

"His present location is unknown," the court document said. "There is no reason to believe that he would respond to a summons."

PART FIVE
TAKING FLIGHT

CHAPTER TWENTY-SEVEN

This time Colton's goal wasn't a burglary. He wasn't hungry for a meal. He didn't want credit cards, cash or a place to shower and sleep. He wasn't looking for an Internet connection to look at porn. This November 11, 2008, Colton was looking for a thrill. He was looking to fulfill a dream. He found what he was looking for in Bob Rivers' 1999 Cessna 182. Colton was going to fly a plane.

Leading up to his first flight, Colton broke into Vern's Bayside and used a stolen credit card to order a DVD on how to fly an airplane. San Juan County sheriff Bill Cumming said there isn't enough evidence to pin the crime on Colton, but the burglary at Vern's is part of the puzzle detectives have pulled together to track Colton.

"We're speaking in terms of truth and legal truth," he said. Truth is what the cops believe Colton did; legal truth is what they can prove in court. "We have a lot of activity that is parallel and similar."

The restaurant's owner said that Colton struck her restaurant twice, once to use a stolen credit card to order the DVD, a second time to take $15,000 in summer profits from the store's safe.

There are several beige hangars on the northeast side of the landing strip. Colton likely cased the area before breaking through the big accordion doors. Once inside, he rifled around looking for keys. Score. In a tackle box in the hangar, Colton found a set that fit Rivers' plane.

He flew the small plane clear across Washington's Cascade mountain range, probably reaching altitudes of more than 7,000 feet, tricky conditions for any novice pilot, never mind someone with no formal training.

Cessna 182s are stable, relatively easy planes to fly. Whether or not Colton had a smooth takeoff isn't known. The flight reportedly was rough, sources told *48 Hours Mystery*. Winds spun the plane upside down. Turbulence caused the plane to dive several thousand feet.

Colton feared he would die. He believed an outside force, a higher power, swooped in and helped him get the plane back under control.

The force didn't help him have a smooth landing.

Bob Rivers remembers the day of Colton's flight. The radio personality talked about the weather on the air. It was gusty and 50 miles per hour winds were forecast, Rivers said. "The pilot in me immediately thought, 'I'm glad I'm not flying in that.' Ironically, about that time my airplane was flying overhead."

Later, when tribal police found the plane crashed at a landing strip at the Yakima Reservation, the only evidence left behind was a cockpit full of vomit. Stomach acid does a number on evidence. Despite trying, scientists couldn't extract enough DNA to determine with certainty that Colton was the felonious pilot.

There were no suspects in the crime for months.

Rivers, a Seattle radio personality at KZOK-FM, said he was shocked when he heard his plane was gone.

"I was called and I couldn't believe it."

CHAPTER TWENTY-EIGHT

Colton's love for planes started at an early age. As a boy, he sketched pictures of planes. He plastered his room with magazine cutouts of jets and told elementary school pals he was going to grow up to be a pilot.

His MySpace page listed "pilot" as his occupation and he reportedly bragged to childhood friends that his father's job was sitting at the controls of an airliner. In grade school, Colton used to bring a photo book of planes, a prized Christmas present, to school, one reporter was told. The boy wanted to talk planes with whoever would listen.

Kohler shared Colton's childhood drawings with national news organizations, licensing the rights to the images. She told me her son loved planes and flying, but confirmed she never paid for formal flying lessons. "He'd never been to flight school," Kohler said.

The closest Colton came, according to his mom, was visiting an exhibit at an aviation museum in Seattle. "He did sit in an airplane twice at the Museum of Flight," she said.

From his backyard, Colton could gaze into the skies and dream of flying. Although Camano Island is remote and rural, some of the world's most advanced jet airplanes soar overhead. Airplane manufacturer Boeing's enormous wide-body production plant is a few miles south across the water at Paine Field in Everett. The giant hulking planes circle over Camano Island on test flights, sometimes before the planes are decorated in the logos of the company's worldwide customers.

Just west of Camano Island, Naval Air Station Whidbey Island in Oak Harbor is home to a fleet of high-powered attack aircraft, the Prowlers and the Growlers. Although these all-weather fighter jets deploy around the globe, they return to Whidbey for maintenance and training. No doubt, these fighters roaring overhead would have captivated the imagination of a young boy with a budding interest in aviation.

CHAPTER TWENTY-NINE

Colton's trip to the Museum of Flight in Seattle would have been a dream come true—that is, if Kohler's story of his visit is accurate. The museum collection includes a 1958 Boeing 707 that at times used the call sign "Air Force One," when Presidents Eisenhower, Kennedy, Johnson and Nixon were aboard. Visitors can walk through the former air-bound presidential office. There's a Concorde, a Lockheed F-104C Starfighter jet and a replica of the original 1903 Wright Flyer. An entire building is dedicated to the early, derring-do fliers of World Wars I and II. Exhibits demonstrate commercial flight control, space exploration and the physics of aviation. Great flying machines of all kinds are suspended from the ceiling in the museum's main gallery. The collection creates a sense of wonder to even the most grounded of visitors.

The history of flight, and the history of the Boeing Company, a business that would shape aviation and the Puget Sound economy, are housed in the Red Barn. The building is the original Boeing airplane-manufacturing plant. The structure was moved to the museum from its original location along the banks of the Duwamish River.

Colton wasn't the first seventeen-year-old flier to capture the region's attention. In 1912, Herb Munter flew a homemade airplane over the waters off Seattle known as Elliott Bay, according to an account by Charlotte D. Widrig. Like Colton, Munter taught himself to fly. Munter and Colton had other similarities. In the days before airports, Munter set his plane down wherever he could find sufficient space, including fairgrounds and cow pastures. And, like Colton, Munter didn't always excel at landing.

Munter was hired in 1915 as a test pilot by an entrepreneur from Detroit named Bill Boeing, a name that would become synonymous with American aviation. Munter, the young test pilot, was put on hold after he twice crashed Boeing's investments, said Tim Detweiler, a flight historian with extensive knowledge of Boeing's life.

Like Colton, Munter survived his crashes. But the early days of aviation are filled with stories with less happy endings. Entrepreneurs perished in the nascent industry. "A lot of people died . . . a lot of the really promising businesses that could have been another Boeing," Detweiler said. "They crashed and killed themselves."

Bill Boeing could have watched Charles Hamilton in 1910 make the first flight over Seattle. On the second or third day of Hamilton's flying shows, while performing the "dive of death," an aerial trick in which the plane stalls and tumbles, he crashed, said Cory Graff. Graff is an aviation historian who now works for the Flying Heritage Collection, owned by Microsoft cofounder Paul Allen. "You've got crashes in the Northwest from the very, very beginning."

Colton also wasn't the first seventeen-year-old to be accused of stealing a plane. Seattle author and airplane historian Steve Ellis dug into his archives and found a note from January 29, 1928. The account, reported in the *Seattle Post-Intelligencer*, was that of a young pilot with no experience who took a floatplane from Lake Washington. The thief hoped to fly the plane all the way across the Canadian border. He didn't get very far. He crashed before leaving Seattle. The would-be pilot told police he was planning to pick up forty cases of bootleg rum.

Colton's dream of flying was well rooted in his surroundings. Plenty of small airfields were at his disposal, many with lax or minimum security, especially once he made his way to the San Juan Islands. Many islanders bypass the ninety-mile drive from Seattle and skip the lineup for the ferry trip. Flying turns a four-hour ordeal into a scenic twenty-minute trip.

CHAPTER THIRTY

Exactly how Colton learned to fly is a mystery that only the now-prisoner can answer. There's evidence he studied flight manuals and Web sites dedicated to flight instruction. People who have both flown and spent time using flight simulator software report that though similar, the two experiences are still remarkably different.

When the news broke that Colton was suspected of stealing planes, his mother at first ridiculed the police. Pam Kohler said her son did not know how to fly an airplane, and she never sent him to flight school. "I know for a fact that he hasn't; I'm his mother," she said. "Let's say you're the smartest person in the world, wouldn't you need a little bit of training in flying a plane? They're not easy."

By October 6, 2009, Kohler told the Associated Press she had rules for Colton's flying. "I hope to hell he stole those airplanes—I would be so proud. But put in there that I want him to wear a parachute the next time."

Learning to fly a plane by reading a manual would be a challenge, experts say. More likely Colton had some type of informal training, said Jim Grant, a flight instructor based in Everett, Washington. Grant believes someone gave Colton a ride and showed him how to fly. After all, Cessna 182s, the model Colton twice stole, are sophisticated planes with complex controls. Flying at higher altitudes over the Cascade range typically takes planning along with skilled navigation.

"I doubt you could actually teach yourself to fly from a flight manual," Grant said.

Microsoft Flight Simulator, a software game that's been on the market for twenty-five years, can create very realistic situations. The latest version, Flight Simulator X, creates "a beautifully rich and realistic world with dozens of aircraft and interactive missions for a completely new and innovative gaming experience. Free flight lets you fly anywhere in the world, from your hometown airport to the most exotic places you've ever dreamed of," states the product's Web site.

"If he had experience with that [software], he probably could fly a light single-engine airplane," said John Frank, the executive director of the Cessna Pilots Association, based in Santa Maria, California.

Still, Frank is skeptical that Colton learned how to fly solely on his own without any guidance. "It would surprise me if he'd never been in an airplane and seen somebody else do it," he said.

Scott Sborov flies small planes for the Washington State Patrol. From the air, troopers hone in on speeding motorists and provide support to the troopers on the ground. The statewide police agency operates a small fleet of fixed-wing aircraft to help keep an eye on the roads. They use sophisticated video equipment to film high-speed encounters, evidence that can be used in court against heavy-footed drivers and hotshots who rev their cars and motorcycles to speeds well over 100 miles per hour.

Sborov, like many pilots, agreed that someone like Colton, with little or no experience, could take off with few problems. The hard part is coming back to earth and setting a plane down. You can't learn to land from reading a book, the trooper said.

"A hard landing would be indicative of someone who hasn't had any flight training or very limited experience," he said.

More likely, Colton wasn't landing as much as he was bringing the plane's altitude to ground level. Landing, even if he ran off the runway and didn't cause a lot of damage, still requires a different set of skills.

"It would be relatively easy for him to get in one of these airplanes, get it started and take off," Frank said. "That's not particularly remarkable."

The 9/11 terrorists who aimed commercial jetliners at New York's World Trade Center towers had no significant flight experience. "They were able to fly those airplanes right into those buildings," Frank said.

Once airborne, it gets easier to direct the plane if the pilot has a rudimentary understanding of global positioning systems. Program in a destination and a computerized autopilot could do most of the work, Frank said. "The airplane will fly there."

At least two of the planes Colton stole were equipped with Garmin GPS systems. Dan DeShon teaches people how to use the Garmin devices. He's also the owner of Westwind Aviation in Friday Harbor, one of the small airports where Colton allegedly stole a plane. DeShon said the equipment is made to be user-friendly and relatively simple. Online tools explain how to manipulate the controls and plot a course. The GPS would help steer the plane and operate it after takeoff, "but it wouldn't really help him with landing," DeShon said.

Maintaining proper altitude is more challenging. Frank believes an examination of Colton's flight patterns would show the aircraft constantly gaining and losing altitude. He said it would be similar to watching a fourteen-year-old drive a car for the first time. "He'd be swerving all over the road," he said.

Accounts of Colton's flight bear this out. Reports derived from radar tracks and other sources show that Colton's flights often were erratic. They must have been terrifying and exhilarating. The adrenaline would have been pumping through him.

Colton was playing an incredibly high-stakes game with his own life and others around him by flying a plane. Many people feared what might happen if he crashed into a school bus or a store full of people. The odds of smashing into another plane, though slim, could have resulted in catastrophic consequences, with more than just Colton's life on the line. "It's breathtaking what the potential for injury is," Sheriff Bill Cumming said.

Colton studied the online flight manuals. He played the video games that simulated flying. He had that childhood love of flight. Colton probably was thinking, "The more I learn, the more I read, the more I want to go out and play," said Mike Rocha, the bounty hunter who later would try to track Colton. Rocha has taken flying lessons himself and believes a student could get almost as much training from software as from a flying instructor. Rocha, like most people familiar with flying, still found it remarkable that Colton would take off and crash five times without killing himself. "That's a huge accomplishment," he said.

CHAPTER THIRTY-ONE

A pilot sitting behind the controls for the first time that early November day in 2008, Colton likely was freaked out. Where to go? Where to land? How to land? These thoughts must have raced through his mind. It's not surprising that he vomited, his stomach retching with fear. If Colton did have a spiritual experience during his first solo flight, it could have been driven by the powerful sensations he would have experienced, including joy and terror.

After crashing Bob Rivers' plane in eastern Washington, Colton reportedly walked for four days before hopping a freight train.

Colton made his way to Reno, Nevada, where he met a friend and used an assumed identity to land a menial job at a casino. After a while, he blew off the job and rode the rails back to Wenatchee, Washington, and then made his way back over the Cascades, back to his home turf on Camano Island.

Not all police departments allow officers to drive patrol vehicles home after a shift, but Island County offered this perk in the summer of 2009. It saves the deputies time, plus they don't need to worry about paying to fill up a tank on their own dime. In rural areas, that can add up.

Rural, remote homes also leave property exposed to prowlers. On June 20, 2009, just before the summer solstice, a deputy and his wife were home. While the couple slept, someone pried open the door on the deputy's patrol vehicle, a Dodge Charger. Once inside the patrol car, the burglar knocked the lock off the department-issued Smith & Wesson rifle that was equipped with a holographic sight. A laptop computer, cell phone and digital camera also were stolen from the car.

"It's unnerving. It's certainly a brazen thing for somebody to do," Island County sheriff Mark Brown said at the time.

All totaled, the thief made off with about six thousand dollars in county property. Police dogs were called in to search the area, but whoever broke into the cop car couldn't be found. The south Camano Island location, the M.O.—it all smelled of Colton. The cops called him a suspect. They were pissed. "It's not something we take lightly," the sheriff said.

As of October 2010, the deputy's property has not been located or returned. No charges have been filed in the car break-in.

CHAPTER THIRTY-TWO

If the dream of flying started in Colton's early youth, the reality began to fill in later, after his escape from Griffin Home. Evidence points to Colton's increasing interest in flying, buying more flight manuals, even ordering a pilot's course.

It wasn't until September 2009, months after Bob Rivers' plane was taken, that detectives connected Colton, an untrained flier and serial burglar, to the plane theft.

A series of events took place the evening of September 11, 2009, that allowed detectives to piece together several crimes they'd been investigating. Colton's second plane theft was the clue that connected him to the plane theft nearly a year before.

As police tell the story, the second theft went down like this: Colton broke into the small airport just outside of Friday Harbor, the small town where the ferries land on San Juan Island. The airport is set on a hill overlooking the harbor. A fence surrounds it. On one end of the runway is the small town. At the other end, the island's rural character takes shape. Deer run nearby. Cows graze.

Detectives believe Colton broke in and got behind the controls of a Cirrus SR22, a small private plane similar to Rivers' Cessna. This time he didn't go far. He reportedly landed the plane with surprising ease just ten miles away as the crow flies, back on Orcas Island. His second piloting experience reportedly took place at night, when flying conditions can be extremely tricky.

Sometime the next day, a cop near Eastsound, on Orcas Island, spotted Colton and gave chase. A sheriff's precinct is nearly adjacent to the small runway. The teen dashed into the woods, and the deputy reportedly said Colton "vaporized." Some reports say that Colton laughed out loud from his hiding place, mocking the deputy.

But then, the heat was on to him and he needed to get away. Far away.

Colton's game of cat and mouse with the cops escalated quickly. He stole a small powerboat from an Orcas Island marina and piloted it through the swift waters of the Salish Sea to Point Roberts, a tiny peninsula with a unique geographical distinction. The northern border, the 49th parallel, is shared with Canada. When driving to Point Roberts from the mainland, people need to cross the international border twice, first to leave the United States and travel about twenty miles across Canadian soil and then cross back into the States. Fire service for the area comes across the border from Canada. The cops hail from the Whatcom County Sheriff's Office.

Sometime around September 22 deputies in Point Roberts began investigating a rash of burglaries. The evidence pointed to Colton. He didn't stick around long. Most likely he stole what he needed and then took off in the first car he could boost.

His trail continued north, about twenty miles, to Vancouver, British Columbia. Vancouver is a magnificent, sprawling metropolis. Towering steel apartment buildings surround the vast harbor. Bridges bring the suburbs to the downtown core. Seaplanes buzz by, whisking passengers to Victoria, the provincial capital, or to Seattle. When Colton passed through, officials were frantically preparing the city for the upcoming Winter

Olympics. Colton didn't stay to enjoy the city's bounty. He snared another luxury car, this time a black BMW, and headed east to Creston, a tiny community about a ten-hour drive east. Until Colton rolled through town, the most recent news about this small corner of British Columbia had been a high-profile polygamy case.

Once in Creston, Colton targeted the Creston Valley Regional Airport. Here he added a dangerous component to his stash of stolen belongings: two handguns. He also grabbed junk food, beer, soda pop and probably scoped out the scene to see if he could steal a plane.

Mary Agnus was the airport's director. "It wasn't Sasquatch," she said. "We didn't see any barefoot prints." It appeared to the locals that there may have been more than one person, although an accomplice was never named.

"I think it's Colton," Agnus told me. The visit from the notorious American didn't sit well with the airport manager. "When somebody is that dangerous and out there, it's pretty scary and puts a lot of panic out there."

Investigators at Creston found a Cessna 182 with a dead battery, a sign that someone may have tried to steal the plane but failed to start it. Frustrated that he couldn't start and steal a Canadian airplane, Colton left and headed south in another stolen car. When he reached the border crossing to get back into the United States, he found it closed to vehicle traffic. The border is closed at 11 p.m.

Colton ditched the stolen car, and evaded U.S. Customs by sneaking across the border to Port Hill, Idaho, where he found another car to steal. From there he headed to the small airport at Bonners Ferry, a town that sprang to life after gold was discovered in the East Kootenays. In 1864, the town's namesake, Edwin Bonner, started running ferry service across the Kootenai River. The ferry is long gone, but the name stuck. When Colton arrived he probably spent about a weekend there, scoping out the scene and assessing the security apparatus at the airport.

Airport officials geared up for a possible prowler. They'd heard about the break-ins north of the border, said Jessica Short, an office manager at the small Idaho landing field. "They called me and said there's some hangars been broken into," she said. "I even went and locked a couple of hangars that were open."

CHAPTER THIRTY-THREE

Pat Gardiner had locked his hangar. That's part of what still irks the retired lawyer who refused to say his exact age but said he's older than seventy. Gardiner runs cattle on acreage in the far northern panhandle of Idaho and used his small plane, a 2005 Cessna Turbo 182, to travel long distances between cattle sales around the region. A Cessna 182 is a solid single-engine plane that typically can cruise at about 125 miles per hour.

Part of what angers Gardiner is that Colton broke into his hangar at the Bonners Ferry Airport not once, but twice. "We didn't think he was going to come back the second time," said Jessica Short, the office manager.

Short said Colton used the airport's bicycle to get around the airfield. He ditched the bike in the mud at the end of a runway. "There was footprints, there was actual footprints leading to a window," she said.

Gardiner said Colton broke into his hangar, tried to pry open the luggage compartment of his plane and then left. Later, police would find barefoot prints on the walls of the airport. They believe Colton put his feet up on the wall while he sat in a chair, relaxing. "There was dirt and food and stuff all over the walls," Short said. Colton used a microwave and left crumbs all over the place.

Gardiner went to the airport to check on things after the first break-in, before his plane was taken. "When I got there, the door had been broken into. The plane was locked and he pried the passenger door open," Gardiner said.

The cattle rancher immediately added a new lock, bolting it directly to the doorframe. But the added security didn't keep Colton out.

"He came back that next night and broke that lock," Gardiner said.

Colton used a screwdriver to break out the key to the starter of Gardiner's plane. Once he was into the electronics, "all he had to do was to turn it to hot," and the plane's engine sprang to life. "He did it without keys. That amazes me, but I don't think it's cool," Short said.

In the middle of the night, Colton broke into Gardiner's hangar and flew the stolen plane back toward western Washington and his home on Camano Island. He could have stolen a car and made the same journey in about a day. Colton was determined to make his third flight.

Gardiner's plane was equipped with a sophisticated tracking device, a Mode-S transponder, that captured information about Colton's longest joyride to date. It's about four hundred miles from northern Idaho to Granite Falls. By the time Colton arrived in airspace that was familiar to him, he would have been extremely low on fuel, Gardiner believes.

Federal investigators shared with Gardiner information about Colton's flight. He flew erratically, "all over the place," the rancher said.

As dawn was breaking in Idaho, Colton fired the engines and took off to the west. Friends of Gardiner later would say they saw the plane struggling to get lift, cruising low over the cornfields and wobbling as it gained elevation. A group of construction workers told Short they saw the plane take off. "Some of them said it sounded like a heavy piece of machinery taking off, sounded a little weird," she said.

Key to Colton's success in flight was his ability to operate a sophisticated piece of electronics in the plane's cockpit. Gardiner had a Garmin G1000, an integrated global positioning system. With a little bit of know-how—and Gardiner believes that Colton stole a manual for the device—it's not that hard to program a flight plan into the computer. Then the GPS would display a map with a rhumb line for the pilot to follow.

Gardiner heard about the plane theft that morning. A friend called him to ask if he'd moved the plane. The rancher said he hadn't.

"Well, your hangar door is open," Gardiner recalls his friend telling him. "Call 911. I'm on my way," the rancher said.

The plane theft set off a flurry of activity. Homeland Security, including ICE, the border patrol arm, federal marshals and the FBI soon descended on Bonners Ferry. Officials at first believed the theft could be linked to terrorism or cross-border drug smuggling. Canadian drug cartels often pilot small planes filled with a valuable cargo of marijuana or Ecstasy. Gardiner said officials told him that if drug runners had stolen his plane, it would likely turn up quickly at a small Canadian airport.

Gardiner's plane wasn't taken by drug smugglers. Colton took it. He flew west over the high desert of eastern Washington, then over the Cascade range. "It's like scary," Short, the airport manager and a novice flier, said. "He would have had to cross mountains and clouds. That's something I wouldn't even do."

Federal officials later would link the teenager to the crime with DNA evidence. The theft would land Colton in the most serious trouble to date. He was charged with taking a plane across state lines, a federal offense. A logger found the wreckage of Gardiner's plane two days after it vanished from Bonners Ferry in a clear-cut in western Washington, not far from Camano Island. Gardiner's insurance company determined the plane was "totaled." It had been valued at around $340,000.

The plane was going nearly 130 miles per hour when it hit the ground. It came to a stop in less than ninety feet, Gardiner said.

That meant the pilot would have experienced up to seven Gs of force on impact. Most roller coasters create about a G-force of four, by comparison. Stunt pilots experience up to twenty Gs when doing tricky maneuvers in air shows. For certain, Colton's stomach must have been in his ears. The landing would have been terrifying.

Clear-cuts are vast swaths of acreage harvested by timber companies. The name conjures images of manicured lawns. In reality, they are anything but. Stumps, fallen logs, brush and new growth make these man-made meadows a harsh environment for a fast-moving plane.

"The thing that saved him is that we had air bags on the plane," Gardiner said. The air bags deployed, allowing Colton to escape from the plane.

He probably crashed around noon on Tuesday, September 29, 2009.

Gardiner believes Colton bolted from the plane's cockpit, perhaps fearing the whole thing would explode. When it didn't, he returned and poured motor oil all over the cockpit, apparently an attempt to conceal fingerprint evidence.

"That is a real congenital criminal," Gardiner said.

CHAPTER THIRTY-FOUR

The crash landing outside Granite Falls was the closest Colton had come to dying, if the wreckage is any indication. He'd put the plane down hard at the same time that his reputation was taking off. The frenzy around Colton Harris-Moore and the Barefoot Bandit was taking flight in the wake of the clear-cut crash.

Two days passed before a logger found the plane's wreckage and called 911. Detectives had a rough time accessing the crash scene in the fading light that evening. The easiest way to get there was up a narrow logging road. Reporters were not allowed close. News helicopters photographed the plane crash from above the following day.

A special team of detectives with the Snohomish County Auto Theft Task Force was sent to investigate. The team focuses on vehicle thefts, including the rare thefts of planes. Special agents from the FBI, who later would take control of the investigation, joined local police.

Speculation soon swirled that barefoot prints were found in the area both at the crash site and back at the airport in Idaho.

"We don't have anything other than his method of operating to indicate that it's him," Boundary County, Idaho, sheriff's detective Dave McClelland said at the time. But, the detective admitted, the incident resembled other Colton crimes. "The methods are very similar." Evidence was later revealed that barefoot prints were seen along a track where Colton likely pushed Gardiner's plane out of a hangar, according to *AOPA Pilot Magazine*.

With a suspect on the run, police often hold back how much evidence they have in a crime scene. It was unlikely McClelland would share all the details as news broke of the theft. "I don't want to say that he is our suspect," McClelland told local papers. "It could be anybody."

Colton's mom was incredulous. She said she didn't know if Colton had taken the flight. If he had, she offered up a suggestion: "I just wish he would wear a parachute." Kohler likened the connection between her son and plane thefts to the way he used to be accused of every burglary on Camano Island. "Now every plane that gets stolen is going to be blamed on him."

Kohler said she hadn't heard from him recently and didn't have control over her son. "I always figured the cops would kill him," Kohler told me at the time. If Colton died, then "that would be what is supposed to happen."

Snohomish County sheriff's spokeswoman Rebecca Hover said the pilot of the crashed Cessna appeared to walk away. "It was obvious that it was a hard landing, but it looked like it was something that someone could survive."

Hover refused to speculate or name possible suspects. As media interest in Colton's case grew, her phone started ringing nonstop with calls from TV news producers in New York. The TV people wanted Hover to appear on national television news shows to discuss the Barefoot Bandit's case. Hover refused. She complained she couldn't get anything else done. Frustrated, Hover set a policy. No one in the Snohomish County Sheriff's Office would affirmatively link the plane crash, or what happened next, to Colton. The rule was that no one would even mention his name to reporters. At the Snohomish County Sheriff's Office, Colton became "He Who Must Not Be Named," a reference to Lord Voldemort, the evil wizard from the popular Harry Potter series. It wasn't until months later, after Colton's arrest in the Bahamas, that I heard Hover speak the name "Colton Harris-Moore."

By now the FBI secretly had joined the effort. The federal agents called Colton a small-time burglar, a local problem. Local police and sheriff's deputies thought he was just a slippery, fast teenager, a harmless kid committing property crimes. So far, Colton hadn't acted violently. That was about to change.

CHAPTER THIRTY-FIVE

Mariah Schroeder was hoping to do her laundry on a sunny fall Monday morning. She set out from her home near Granite Falls, a small town saddled between suburbs to the west and the Cascades to the east. Granite Falls is the gateway to the Mountain Loop Highway, a fifty-mile circuit over Barlow Pass. The road offers access to some of the most concentrated networks of hiking trails in the Pacific Northwest. Some routes climb Mount Pilchuck, a 5,324-foot peak that towers over the town. Other trails lead up Three Fingers, another mountain peak, and to the east there's access to Glacier Peak, one of the region's sleeping volcanoes.

Schroeder wasn't setting out to hike that day, October 6, 2009. She went into the town to run errands and by the time she returned, police cars blocked her way. "I can't get home," she said.

Scores of heavily armed cops made their way up Highway 92 to Granite Falls that morning. A Black Hawk helicopter swirled its blades above. Late the night before, homeowners discovered that they'd been burglarized. The latest break-in had all the signs of Colton. Missing from the home were blankets, food and, notably, a pair of shoes. A firearm also was taken.

The cops went into the dark woods hunting their suspect. Near the home, and about three and a half miles from where the plane crashed, the deputies found a campsite, according to federal court records. Among the items scattered in the woods was a .32-caliber pistol stolen a few days earlier from Creston, British Columbia.

What happened next is one of the most violent episodes in Colton's drama. Court records simply say, "As police searched the area near the campsite, a shot was fired by an unknown individual in the woods." Officials have told me off the record that there's not enough evidence to pin the assault on Colton, but there is little doubt it was he. Fingerprints recovered from the campsite matched Colton's. Additionally, despite Colton's efforts to destroy evidence in the wreckage of Gardiner's plane, investigators found enough DNA to link him to the theft.

Many scenarios can unfold when someone fires a weapon at a police officer. Rarely do events transpire as they do in television dramas or in Hollywood films. Police want to finish their shifts in one piece and return home to their families. First and foremost in their minds is their own safety, and the safety of the other cops working with them.

Colton likely believed, "If I pop a round off, they bed and wait," one law enforcement official told me.

Gunfire changed a burglary investigation into a tense manhunt for a potentially armed and very dangerous suspect.

"That took it up several notches," Hover, the local police spokeswoman, said.

The rural area where Colton had set up camp sits on unincorporated county land about five miles outside the city of Granite Falls. County deputies were the cops who heard the bullet whiz by. Police from around the region responded.

Teams trained in special weapons and tactics, better known as SWAT, were called out. Dozens of police carrying automatic rifles and dressed in camouflage fatigues raced to the scene. Time was of the essence. Everyone knew Colton was fast. His heart must have been racing after he fired the pistol. He bolted away through the brush.

A Black Hawk helicopter, an asset of the U.S. Department of Homeland Security, used sophisticated electronics and heat-seeking radar to catch glimpses of life through the dense tree canopy. The commotion woke up Bob and Eva Clemence. Outside the couple's home in a small subdivision deputies raced up and down the streets in their patrol cars. In the quiet of the pre-dawn morning, neighbors said they could hear the cops mention a single suspect's name: "Colton."

"If he's brazen enough to shoot at a police officer—that makes you a little leery," Bob Clemence said.

The county's team of major crime detectives huddled around a conference table inside Granite Falls' small police station. While Hover, the spokeswoman, skirted the issue of Colton with reporters, the detectives were reviewing his files, talking with cops from around the region, trying to flesh out where he might go and how to intercept him. The FBI took a seat at the table.

To the cops, this was serious business. Colton was risking his life and the lives of officers, and distracting resources from other pressing issues. Specially trained man-trackers followed Colton's footprints through the woods. They looked for broken branches, disturbed leaves and other clues to follow his path. But the path went cold.

By the time the sun began to set, the SWAT teams were called off and the units sent back to their shifts. "We're going to keep going until we either arrest this person or can say with some degree of certainty that the suspect isn't there anymore," Hover said.

Once again, Colton had vaporized, disappeared just beyond the grasp of law enforcement.

Andrew Vachss, the lawyer and child advocate, is quick to point out that Colton's alleged crimes, while numerous, likely could not be proven to be violent. I asked Vachss about the incident near Granite Falls when Colton was rumored to have "possibly" shot a weapon at a deputy.

"They're not charging, I don't think you can say 'possibly,'" Vachss pointed out. Investigators would have combed the area for enough evidence to bring the assault to trial. Trying to murder a cop is a heinous crime, not a childish prank. Vachss was highly skeptical about the incident. Criminals operate in patterns, he said. And Colton's pattern was burglary and theft, not rape, murder or assault.

There are reports of another incident involving Colton and a deputy, the details of which are even sketchier than the reported gunfire near Granite Falls. Pepper spray was used by a suspect in an incident with a San Juan County sheriff's deputy. Sources within law enforcement suggested Colton was responsible. San Juan County sheriff Bill Cumming said there wasn't enough evidence to link the assault to Colton.

If Colton thought he was playing a game with the cops, the violent turn near the camp in Granite Falls removed any humor from police working the case.

CHAPTER THIRTY-SIX

Zack Sestak first read about Colton in a local paper. Sestak, a writer in his mid-twenties, was fascinated with the story. He liked Colton's bravado, the way he was sticking it to the man.

"He's becoming a folk hero to a lot of people," Sestak said.

What Sestak did to celebrate Colton was simple. A few keystrokes and clicks of a computer mouse. It was done. In early October 2009 Sestak started a Facebook fan page to follow Colton's exploits.

"It started kind of as a joke," he said. It was fantastic that an untrained teenager had piloted stolen planes, not once, but several times.

"This is unheard of," Sestak said. "It's a story that's completely different."

He called Colton's behavior crazy and bizarre, but at the same time inspiring.

"If we all had that kind of balls, who knows what the world would be like," Sestak said.

As the story continued to gain momentum, Sestak became the voice for people who supported Colton. Soon, other fans clicked on the Web site to join. First they were numbered in the hundreds, then thousands, then tens of thousands. By the end of Colton's run, hundreds of thousands of people claimed to be his fans.

Sestak likened Colton to a modern-day Jesse James—minus the murders. "Do I hope he gets caught? I wouldn't really wish that on anybody," Sestak said at the time. "It's a fun story, because of the nature of what he's doing." Colton had victims, Sestak admitted, but he rarely was known to cause physical harm. Instead he was breaking into multimillion-dollar homes and stealing from people at a time when Wall Street executives were receiving huge payouts for failing at their jobs. Not that Colton was victimless, Sestak said. No one asked to be a part of the story. The writer, who since has moved from the Pacific Northwest to San Diego, himself has been burglarized. His laptop was taken. "That's kind of a fact of life. People steal and people get stolen from," he said.

"This isn't essentially a new story, it's a story that's been retold," Sestak said. "Colton's just the latest installment with a little different twist." On the Facebook page, Sestak urged Colton to stay one step ahead of the cops: "Let's hope that he remains healthy, free and at large for a long time! Fly, Colton, Fly!"

Sestak has his own history that, in part, helped him feel empathy for Colton. After graduating from Kamiak High School, Sestak was hit by a car and lost much of his memory. He left the hospital with a bag full of painkillers that led him on a path to drug abuse. "It took me down a very difficult road," he said.

Like Colton, Sestak had his own experiences trying to outrun the law. He could understand a bit of what Colton was going through. "The feeling of being on the run is something that I know pretty well," Sestak said.

Colton gave voice to people who were fed up with and let down by the system, Sestak said. People who were broke and broken. "Whether or not he was taking on the system and winning, that's what people perceived in him," Sestak said. "He was the right outlaw at the right time."

As quickly as Sestak's Facebook page gained popularity, others joined the fray to get in on the bazaar that was springing up around Colton. Like Sestak, Seattle T-shirt artist Adin Stevens dug what Colton was doing. He sat down and morphed Colton's already iconic self-portrait into a spoof. He Photoshopped the image, and then borrowed a line from Merle Haggard's famous song "Mama Tried." The T-shirt said "Momma Tried, Colton Harris-Moore Fan Club" and featured a black-and-white mug shot, the self portrait of the infamous Barefoot Bandit. (Given Kohler's history with Colton, the T-shirts could have more accurately read "Momma Didn't Try.")

"He's pretty gangster," Stevens said. "It's rad to see a kid his age going for it."

At Good Times Printing in Seattle, orders for Colton T-shirts started flooding in from around the country, Stevens said. Within days Stevens was printing as many shirts as he could. He vowed to donate a portion of his earnings to a charity for troubled youth.

"I sold a couple hundred bucks' worth this morning," he said at the time. "With all the interest, I was forced to think about why I wanted to make the shirts. I really don't know, to be honest. I just think it's an extraordinary story. I can relate to Colton in a number of ways. It's a good outlaw story. . . . I had my share of trouble growing up."

Fueled by Sestak, Stevens and others, Colton's story took on a life of its own. The tale of a teenager who ran barefoot through the woods, stole planes and managed time and again to escape capture quickly became fodder for national news programs.

Before the week was out, many people close to the story,

myself included, were invited to speak on national news shows. Colton's ascension to national folk hero occurred despite strong voices opposed to his glorification, especially the people whose job it was to apprehend the fugitive.

"To glamorize him as a folk hero is wrong," San Juan County sheriff William Cumming said. "He should be characterized for what he is. He's a serial burglar. He's a thief, and he obviously has a lot of turmoil in his life, and that's not something to glamorize."

Bob Rivers, the Seattle radio host whose plane Colton allegedly stole, decided to share his story publicly, hoping the added press interest would help catch the fugitive. Rivers already was worried that Colton's legend was outpacing reality. "I'm not a fan of the media frenzy because I don't like the whole cult hero thing," he said. "But if keeping it alive helps solve it, then I think it's worth it."

Rivers appeared on a nationally broadcast Fox News interview with Pam Kohler. Among colorful comments such as, "I told him to start taking parachutes," Kohler urged Colton to give up.

"It's not my place to judge anyone," Rivers said afterward. "I'm told he had a difficult childhood. The only thing I agreed with her on is she would like him to turn himself in."

As the storm of media interest grew, Mark Brown, the Island County sheriff, said he was working closely with other police agencies. He was staying true to the job of ending Colton's run. "I hope he's caught and I hope he goes to prison for this," the sheriff said. "Hopefully, we'll catch the guy."

But the legend grew. Soon the fine line between fact and fiction started to blur as Colton's tale was told and retold. In the coming weeks, television crews from as far away as Brazil crossed the Mark Clark Bridge to film the outside of Colton's child-

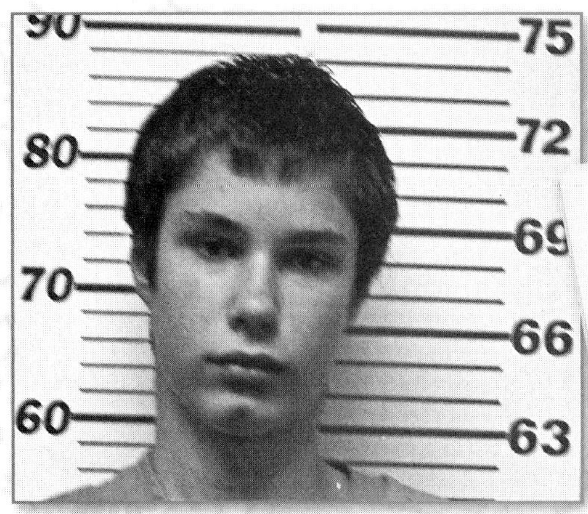

Colton Harris-Moore, 15. This booking photo was distributed in 2007 by the Island County Sheriff's Office.

Photo by the Island County Sheriff's Office

Photo by Kevin Nortz, *The Herald of Everett*

Colton Harris-Moore, 15, sits in a Coupeville courtroom for a bail hearing after his arrest in February 2007. Deputies had been trying to capture him for six months.

Newly elected Island County sheriff Mark Brown met with Camano Island residents in February 2007. He's shown here holding a wanted poster for Colton's accomplice and self-described criminal mentor, Harley Davidson Ironwing. Ironwing surrendered to police after Colton was arrested.

Photo by Jennifer Buchanan, *The Herald of Everett*

Colton Harris-Moore, 16. Police released this November 2007 photo after Colton escaped from a group home in April 2008.

Photo by the Island County Sheriff's Office

oto by the Island County Sheriff's Office

Mom,
cops were here
everythings on lockdown
I'm leaving 4-wennachi
wont Be Back Est. 2 mont
I'll contact you they
took well I'm going to
have my afilliates take
Care of that.
P.S - cops wana play
hu!? well its not
no lil game ..... It's
war!
& tell them that

Colton left this note for his mother after a police raid in September 2006. He had a message for the authorities: "This is war."

Photo by the Washington State Department of Corrections

Gordon Moore, Colton's father, in a 1999 booking photo.

Photo by the Washington State Department of Corrections

Harley Davidson Ironwing seen in a booking photo.

Colton took this self-portrait on July 8, 2008. The Island County Sheriff's Office released the photo later that month.

Photo courtesy of the Island County Sheriff's Office

SWAT teams looked for Colton near Granite Falls, Washington, in October 2009 after a gun was fired at deputies investigating a burglary. Colton had crashed a plane nearby days earlier.

Photo by Mark Mulligan, *The Herald of Everett*

Photo by Mark Mulligan, *The Herald of Everett*

Colton slipped away from heavily armed teams of law enforcement several times. Teams from the FBI, Homeland Security, the U.S. Coast Guard, and several local sheriff's offices hunted for him on Turtleback Mountain in March 2010 after a homeowner spied the elusive fugitive.

Photo by Elizabeth Armstrong, *The Herald of Everett*

Camano Island resident Major Freeman asked a bounty hunter about a wanted poster of Colton during a June 2010 community meeting about the fugitive. Hundreds of people turned out to talk about the island's notorious son.

Bounty hunter Mike Rocha joined the effort to arrest Colton in May 2010. He's seen here talking to Camano Island residents at a community meeting in early June.

Photo by Elizabeth Armstrong, *The Herald of Everett*

Richard Grover said he used a dowsing rod to try to find Colton. He's shown here along Camano Ridge Road near a barn where he believed Colton was hiding. Colton actually was hundreds of miles away on his way to the Bahamas at the time.

Photo by Mark Mulligan, *The Herald of Everett*

Joshua Flickner, manager of the Elger Bay Grocery, became a defacto spokesman for Camano Island residents angry that Colton became a national folk hero. He spoke to reporters after Colton was arrested.

Photo by Jennifer Buchanan, *The Herald of Everett*

Don McLain, manager of Tyee Grocery on south Camano Island, showed off his "Colton's Corner." Colton was accused of breaking into the store as a teen. Now the store features Colton in a series of posters.

to by Jennifer Buchanan, *The Herald of Everett*

Photo by Jennifer Buchanan, *The Herald of Everett*

Camano Island residents created spoofs of Colton that were displayed at the Tyee Grocery. The newest poster, created hours after Colton's arrest, showed him wearing prison garb and said, "Greetings from Camano Island. Welcome back, Colt!"

Renowned Seattle defense attorney John Henr Browne speaks with reporters after Colton's firs Seattle court appearance in June 2010. Browne said Colton didn't enjoy his years on the run and didn't want to be considered a role model.

Photo by Mark Mulligan, *The Herald of Everett*

hood home. The Brazilian news reporter, unsure of what might happen if she knocked on the door, called me to ask if I thought Kohler would shoot her. The reporter never did get her interview with Colton's mother.

Kohler put up a sign at the end of her driveway warning trespassers they would be shot. A CBS News crew was filming when they approached her mobile home one afternoon. She met the three-person crew with threats and they backed off as she went to fetch her shotgun. She later relented and talked to the crew off-camera.

It didn't matter that Kohler didn't want to be interviewed. Colton's tale had a life of its own. A story with the headline "The Legend of Colt" appeared on the October 9, 2009, front page of the *Globe and Mail*, a national Canadian newspaper. Canada's leading television newsmagazine, *The Nation*, filmed a segment about the teen. He appeared in national newspapers in Great Britain, including *The Guardian*.

"[He is] not this myth they're trying to make him into," Island County sheriff's detective Ed Wallace said. "He's a criminal stealing for his own gratification—either for the property or the thrill, I can't answer that."

Wallace tried to distinguish Colton from other criminal folk heroes: Colton didn't steal from the rich to give to the poor. He didn't rob banks or trains. He was never a detective or a spy. He wasn't a fictional superhero, either, and he didn't have an invisibility cloak.

It didn't matter. For many Colton did what wasn't being done.

"I looked at the guy as somewhat of a hero," said Bill Moody, a builder who lives on Lopez Island. "He was outsmarting our [police] intelligence. He was doing it in a way that wasn't harming anybody, a peaceful warrior marching to his own beat."

Shortly after Colton's arrest in the Bahamas, a person who went by the name Jimmy Dean posted an online comment in reference to one of my stories published in the *Herald*. "Colton is a hero to many of our children," the man wrote. "In a day and age when sports stars are beating their wives and movie stars are going to jail for drugs and [drunken driving], Colton is a breath of fresh air. My children love Colton and want to meet him. They think he is a true survivalist and talk about him nonstop."

CHAPTER THIRTY-SEVEN

In short order, Colton became an American outlaw folk hero. The teenager morphed into something bigger than himself. He was fitting into an archetype few have stepped into.

A few months after Colton's arrest, I reached Sharon Sherman and asked her to take a fresh look at the Barefoot Bandit's story. The professor of folklore at the University of Oregon in Eugene likened Colton's saga to the stories of Bonnie and Clyde, Pretty Boy Floyd and other infamous crooks.

"What happens is we expurgate anything we don't like about those people and we input anything we like," she said. "It becomes what we want to hear."

It's what happened with Jesse James in the nineteenth century. In the twentieth century, there were Bonnie and Clyde and John Dillinger.

There also was another infamous Northwest criminal who, like Colton, will forever be linked to airplanes. He said his name was Dan Cooper, although the media dubbed him D.B. FBI officials still haven't determined his true identity. On November 24, 1971, D.B. Cooper boarded a Seattle-bound plane in Portland, Oregon. He paid for his seat in cash and, once seated, ordered a bourbon and soda before takeoff. With the flight airborne, Cooper handed a flight attendant a note that said he had a bomb in his briefcase; then he slipped her a note demanding $200,000 and four parachutes.

Cooper's plane landed in Seattle and he traded the passengers for the cash, delivered in twenty-dollar bills, and the silk parachutes. The plane departed and, around 8 p.m., somewhere between Seattle and Reno, Cooper jumped out of the back of the plane with the money. At first officials figured he was an experienced skydiver, although that later turned out to be just a rumor. Over the years there have been theories and deadends, but never an arrest. Cooper is wanted by the FBI to this day. The case remains unsolved.

Even though Cooper made off with thousands of dollars and put lives at risk, he entered the American imagination of what was possible. In the end, like Colton, no other lives were lost. Whether Cooper survived his daring dive, only Cooper knows.

Another piece of Colton's story that helped him take on greater dimensions were the odds he had to overcome, Sherman said. In Colton's case, it was his abusive upbringing, his lack of formal education and the dozens, perhaps hundreds of police who wanted nothing better than to bring him down.

Then there was his bravado. His flair. The way Colton stuck it to the man. "In some ways the outlaw hero does something we'd want to do ourselves," Sherman said.

Colton thumbed his nose at the cops. He targeted the wealthy, played in their homes and used their toys, during the worst economic times in decades.

"He's actually doing what he wished he could do," Sherman said. "After a while you get people cheering you on."

Of course, Colton had the added benefit of the devoted following on Facebook. Sherman said the lightning-fast quality of the Internet propelled Colton into the mass media, fueling his rise from local hero to national and international fame.

The Internet was to Colton what photographs were to Bonnie and Clyde. Bonnie Parker and Clyde Barrow became household names during the Great Depression and the era of the "public enemy." Together the pair were believed to have killed nine police officers and many more bystanders. The couple was killed in a police shoot-out on May 23, 1934. Other outlaw folk heroes came before the murderous couple, but never before had newspapers had access to such striking photos, which Bonnie and Clyde left behind. Bonnie's sex appeal, a photo of her holding a gun, smoking a cigar, helped fuel the interest. The appeal of those photographs helped transform the bank robbers into a national sensation.

Facebook did the same for Colton. When the Island County Sheriff's Office released his self-portrait, his smirking face nestled among the ferns, the photo helped fan the flames of Colton's fame. The photograph was beamed on cable news programs and news wires around the world. It was the image Stevens used to create his T-shirts. *Outside* magazine, which ran a feature story on Colton, used the image to create an artist's montage.

Colton did what most people wouldn't dare do. He taunted law enforcement and played an ongoing game of cat and mouse. His fans looked past his wrongdoings. They applauded Colton's fuck-it-all ambition.

"Catch me, if you can," Colton was saying, Sherman believes. "Can you catch me? That's part of the 'Ha ha, I pulled this off right under your nose.' "

Andrew Vachss, the child advocate and lawyer, believes that Colton may have found the Facebook attention as alluring as the adrenaline he experienced in flying. People online liked him, praised him, actually understood and listened to him. There were thousands cheering him to fly on and keep going. "That could be very, very addictive," Vachss said.

Harold Schechter, a professor of American literature at Queens College at the City University of New York, has written widely about American outlaws, including several historical accounts of some of America's worst criminals. To understand bad guys from a cultural perspective, it's important to look at the driving psychological motivation, he said.

"Any system of morality to which we subscribe becomes oppressive to us. We also have this wild, lawless side that needs to find expression." The oppressed side needs an outlet, a voice and balance. Expression is found vicariously through the outlaw folk hero. "It's something very, very fundamental in the human imagination that needs these stories," Schechter said.

Throughout history, the character of the "trickster" has been repeated in spoken and written lore. Time and again fictional, mythological and real characters fulfill the public's appetite for the bad-guy hero.

"The interesting thing, since there are many lawbreakers, why is it that one particular character will capture the imagination? Why the Barefoot Bandit?" Schechter wondered.

Although some people, including Sestak, suggest that Colton was distinguished because he didn't physically harm his victims, Schechter doesn't buy that.

John Dillinger, Al Capone, and Bonnie and Clyde all committed horrific violence and still became mythic characters in American lore. Though Colton's taste for property crimes over violent crimes may have appeased the conscience of some of his followers, his ascension to hero status came from his flair and style, Schechter said.

Colton's boyish good looks gave him a bad-boy debonair aura that surely must have resonated with the thousands who cheered for him to keep running. He later would leave messages, sign notes using his moniker the Barefoot Bandit, and live up to the nickname, making getaways in bare feet. It helped that Colton carried off the crimes with panache, Schechter said.

"Even the fact that he could be labeled with this tabloid nickname adds to the whole mystique." Add Colton's insouciance and the coolness of his character, and he fits nicely into the archetype. That myth, Schechter said, is constantly being reinvented to resonate with the particular cultural moment.

Colton committed his "trickster" crimes during a time when foreclosures were at a high, when people were unemployed by the tens of thousands and economic uncertainty was rampant.

"It was like the perfect storm," said Mike Rocha, the bounty hunter who would soon join in the chase. "Time in society was right."

The underdog became the hero. "He stepped into the limelight at just the exact right time," Rocha said.

CHAPTER THIRTY-EIGHT

Harley Davidson Ironwing was nearing the end of his thirty-three-month prison term for attempting to steal from the Stanwood church.

Weeks earlier, Harley was transferred from the Washington Corrections Center in Shelton, Washington, to the Bishop Lewis Work Release Program near Seattle, a Department of Corrections spokesman told me. Prisoners earn work release privileges through good behavior. The concept is to help prisoners gain job skills to smooth the transition back into society after they are released.

Harley got dressed to go to a job interview on a late-October day in 2009. He left the halfway house where he was assigned, took the bus and didn't come back. Six days later, Everett police nabbed Harley for allegedly shoplifting at the mall.

Pam Kohler told me she never much liked Harley. Now she mocked the man who claimed to be her famous son's mentor. "Maybe Colt can teach him how to escape and not get caught," Kohler said. "A favor for a favor."

While Colton stayed hidden, Boeing debuted its newest jumbo jet, the highly fuel-efficient and modern 787 Dreamliner. Huge crowds gathered on December 16, 2009, at Paine

Field in Everett to watch the new jet make its inaugural flight. Extra security was on hand. Some people joked the security presence was to prevent Colton from sneaking in and taking the controls.

The sleek new jetliner swiftly took off for her maiden voyage, running test patterns. Colton clearly wasn't in control. The pilots set the plane down beautifully at Boeing Field, just south of Seattle.

Colton's story was gaining more and more attention. *Time* magazine named Colton "America's Most Wanted Teenage Bandit" in its December 21, 2009, issue. The tale of the Barefoot Bandit was sinking into the American mind-set like bare feet in the sand. The imprint of Colton's mug and the story of the down-and-out kid who taught himself to fly stolen planes was soaring.

Pam Kohler told me she was growing weary of being bothered by reporters at her home. She accused the cops, the media and people on the Internet of exaggerating her son's behavior. "He doesn't live outside. He lives in a home, has his own room," she repeated. She said she spoke to him occasionally over an untraceable phone line and didn't know his location. She was convinced that Colton's phone was similar to one used by the president of the United States. The line was impenetrable, she said.

For her part, Kohler said she changed her phone number more than once, in part to prevent the cops from listening in and to dissuade nosy reporters from invading her privacy. Colton's popularity on the Internet was drawing more and more people to the story.

"He thinks that Facebook is funny, with all his followers," Kohler said. As the Christmas holiday approached, I called

Kohler to ask what was on her mind, if she would be buying Colton any gifts. She wanted her son to be prepared for a confrontation with the cops. She did have something on her list for Colton.

"A bulletproof vest," she said.

CHAPTER THIRTY-NINE

Colton made his way back to Orcas Island. There was a bizarre and telling message scrawled in chalk across the red-painted concrete floor of Kyle Ater's Homegrown Market and Gourmet Deli. Thirty-nine large, well-drawn outlines of bare feet led a path across the floor. Five little toes were carefully drawn at the top of each foot. The drawings wound through the store's aisles and then led to a side door. At the exit, the intruder wrote a message to accompany the collection of cartoonlike feet. He wrote, "Cya."

"It was an art project," Ater said.

Overnight, someone had used a pry bar to break into the small organic grocery store. The place was ransacked. Whoever it was grabbed twelve hundred dollars in cash. The burglar destroyed the computerized security system and helped himself to mounds of organic food, including a blueberry cheesecake. The big stainless steel kitchen sink behind the deli counter was running, overflowing water when Ater arrived. In the deep sink, the intruder left the computer system, an effort to wash away any evidence that might have been captured by the surveillance system.

The burglar raided the produce section and left the dessert case empty. He grabbed several trays of unbaked meat-and-cheese croissants, the buttery dough patiently rising.

It wasn't even 8:30 a.m. that February morning.

Ater called 911 and San Juan County sheriff's deputies responded to investigate the mess. Before the deputy could finish his work, news of another crime was broadcast over the dispatch radio. A plane stolen from Anacortes was found in the mud off the landing strip, less than a mile from Ater's store. Right then, Ater said he knew it was Colton.

"As soon as we got the call, that's it, it was confirmation. That's his M.O.," Ater said. His heart sank. He was furious. The grocery store owner said he wouldn't hesitate to help someone in need, but this brazen burglary threatened Ater's business and his employees' jobs. "I'm the most peaceful person on the planet," Ater said, "but I have twenty people relying on me to run my biz and this is exactly what I feared."

Beatrice von Tobel spotted the plane when she arrived for work that morning at the Orcas Island Airport. She's the airport manager and the sole employee of the Port of Orcas, one of two public port commissions in Washington whose lone responsibility is operating a small island airport. The other is on nearby Lopez Island.

Von Tobel, who goes by Bea, at first worried someone was hurt when she saw the plane off the north end of the runway. Then she saw the type of plane. "Oh shit, it's a Cirrus." The plane was a Cirrus SR22, the same model Colton previously had taken from Friday Harbor and crashed at the other end of the Orcas runway. At least this time, Colton didn't take out a runway light, von Tobel said.

While von Tobel and Ater were convinced that Colton was the culprit, the cops wouldn't confirm their suspicions. San Juan County sheriff Bill Cumming would only say that Colton was a "strong person of interest." "We are operating as though he is still in our jurisdiction and planning our operational steps accordingly."

Aviation officials had spotted the plane near Orcas Island just before midnight. The radar track showed it flying erratically; the altitude and course were "all over the place," von Tobel said. Remarkably, the pilot landed the plane with little damage. He'd been aloft for about ten minutes.

As usual, Colton left behind plenty of evidence to piece together what happened. He'd broken into a hangar at the Anacortes Airport, a small private field back on the mainland. The small airport is just minutes from the busy ferry landing that shuttles residents back and forth to the islands. He must have slipped into the plane's cockpit sometime before midnight and then made the short flight to Orcas. At night, he would have been forced to use the plane's GPS and instruments. Flying at night is far more complex than daylight flying. Most pilots rely on IFR—instrument flight rule—to guide the aircraft without daytime cues to help. But IFR would have required hours and hours of study and Colton more likely turned on the GPS and used his knowledge of the area's topography and waterways to guide him.

From the air, Orcas is easy to pick out. Mount Constitution's peak rises high above any other natural feature in the San Juan Islands archipelago. The summit is studded with blinking lights atop towers that could have helped Colton find his way. The runway lights at the Port of Orcas operate all night to guide pilots in, von Tobel said.

During the day, von Tobel keeps an eye on the runway from her office, often with the help of Suka, a big black Lab. Together, they showed me where on the runway Colton had landed. The runway tour served a dual purpose of chasing off about a half-dozen Canada geese that were feeding dangerously close to the tarmac. The airport manager brought three shells, a banger, screamer and whizzler, and more than enough gun powder to startle the geese and move the birds on to other pastures.

Von Tobel is a pragmatic person. She answered my questions while keeping busy with her work. I tagged along with her while she ran her Friday afternoon errands to the post office and the bank, the same one Colton allegedly broke into. Colton has chutzpah, she said. He displayed intelligence without being smart. He knew enough to find people's hidden keys but not enough to give up or to do better for himself.

Even months after his arrest, island gossip persists about Colton. Von Tobel believed he must have had help, but no one's been identified. After the crash, officials found a den Colton created for himself in the rafters of an airplane hangar. It was the same hangar used by state investigators to comb the plane Colton crashed for evidence. Colton may have been watching the Washington State Patrol crime lab technicians at work, von Tobel said.

The fastidious owner of the hangar found a flight manual on the passenger seat of his aircraft one day. The out-of-place manual was unusual because the pilot never left things out of place, von Tobel said. Colton likely was studying flying as he lived in the hangar's rafters.

If he wasn't in the hangar, he could have been anywhere on Orcas. "There's a lot of places to hide here," she said. Each fall, the island rises out of the water like Brigadoon. "So many people are seasonal. This time of year it's kind of like lemmings," she said. Summer residents flee to warmer climates in Southern California and Arizona. The population takes a nosedive. "There are fewer people here."

Left behind are empty vacation homes, just like Colton had found available for his use on Camano Island. Von Tobel said she couldn't imagine what it must have been like for

Colton to be alone for so long. "It surely would have been a lonely life."

After crashing the Cirrus, Colton easily could have hopped the eight-foot-tall field fence that surrounds the Orcas Island landing field. The runway used to be surrounded by a few strings of barbed wire, but a collision between a deer and a plane sometime in the early 2000s convinced the locals to have their view of the landing field interrupted by the taller fence, von Tobel said.

The night of Colton's short flight to Orcas Island, federal aviation officials noticed the Cirrus SR22 on radar. Preparations were under way for the Winter Olympics in nearby Vancouver, British Columbia. Airspace in the region had been restricted. At first questions were raised about whether Colton violated the Olympic no-fly zone stretching south from Canada. Officials later acknowledged that the plane merely skirted the boundary. There was something else, though, that struck officials as odd. The plane was sending out the wrong transponder code.

Colton also left a fingerprint on the aileron and a note to himself in the cockpit. Prosecutors later used this evidence to charge him with breaking into the hangar and stealing the plane.

They were mistakes, but not enough to get Colton caught. By the time officials put the pieces together, Colton again had vanished. Police scoured the area looking for Colton. Once officials realized the suspect was cornered on an island, they sent out reinforcements hoping this episode would be his last. Ater said deputies at first weren't terribly interested in collecting evidence from the burglary. Once Colton surfaced as a suspect, specially trained technicians were called in from the mainland. The manhunt was on, but the manhunt didn't flush out the target. Colton continued to run.

After the burglary, Ater resorted to a different type of

security system. Later in the week, Ater slept in the store's office with a gun and his two big dogs, a Rottweiler and a yellow Labrador, by his side. The system may not have been high-tech, but it was sound. The whole experience irked Ater. After Colton had prowled Eastsound the previous summer, Ater invested thousands of dollars to put in a sophisticated surveillance system with a dozen cameras. Each was capable of taking images in the dark and snapping thirty frames each second. He purchased the electronic security with Colton in mind.

"The only reason I bought that security system was for him," Ater said. "So I could go home and sleep."

Ater was convinced Colton had broken into the store years before, in late summer 2006, right after Ater purchased the business. The M.O. was exactly the same. Ater said it was a nearly identical crime, minus the art project of chalk drawings.

The timing of the 2006 burglary would have been right for Colton. At the time, Colton was on the run and suspected in break-ins closer to his home on Camano Island. It's possible he made his way to Orcas Island. Colton wasn't on the radar of the San Juan County Sheriff's Office then. Authorities blamed the 2006 break-in on a local kid, Ater said. For Ater, it was an insurance claim. Now, the 2006 burglary haunts the store owner. He can't figure out why Colton taunted him.

After the burglary that February in 2010, Ater turned the soggy computer over to the authorities, hoping they could extract data from the waterlogged hard drive. Months later, I stopped in to see Ater. He was busy making lunch salads. The chalk marks were long gone, but Ater still was talking about Colton. The computer still hadn't turned up images of Colton—or anyone for that matter. But it wasn't for a lack of trying. Ater was waiting to hear back from producers at CBS

News who had taken the computer in hopes of extracting a few glimpses of Colton.

By October, nine months after Colton allegedly drew the chalk drawings on Ater's floor, Ater said he'd heard nothing from prosecutors. Deputies had stopped by the store to ask Ater to identify a $350 drill, a piece of evidence the deputies were keeping in case it was needed at a trial. Ater just wants the drill back.

As months stretched on and Colton was still loose, police conducted search after search on the island. As helicopters whirled their blades over the small town of Eastsound, Ater joined other islanders in front of his grocery store to watch as heavily armed police scoured the otherwise bucolic area.

"We were all just out there like the circus," Ater said.

The tally of stolen property, planes, jewelry, electronics, insurance claims and damage attributed to Colton by now totaled about $1.5 million.

As stories of fantastic getaways continued to make national headlines, I believed it was important to bring a focus to the people being victimized, people like Kyle Ater, whose business nearly was ruined.

"This is not Robin Hood," Island County sheriff's detective Ed Wallace said. "He's stealing for his own gratification, and he's hurting people."

Ater was out more than five thousand dollars, a dent he feared could force layoffs or other drastic measures. "This is such a huge attack. It's not just financial, it's emotional," he said.

Many of Harris-Moore's victims had insurance and some stolen property was returned. Still, people had to pay deductibles and deal with the hassle of canceling credit cards and filing claims. More upsetting, though, was the violation so many people experienced from having their homes, their sanctuaries of safety, defiled. "That's the biggest loss," Detective Wallace said. "No amount of restitution can bring that feeling of safety back."

Bob Rivers, the Seattle talk-radio host whose plane was stolen, told me his community on Orcas Island had changed since Colton arrived. By this time Rivers had been interviewed by national news programs about Colton. The story of the Barefoot Bandit was becoming increasingly sensational, fueling Colton's status as an outlaw folk hero. "Am I helping to catch this guy or helping to get out a delusion?" Rivers wondered. "He's shitting all over other people's lives."

Ater could only guess where Colton ran off to or what tree he was hiding under. Orcas might be an island, but there are plenty of hiding places, scores of vacation homes, nooks in outbuildings and other out-of-the-way places for a fugitive to lurk. Still, the night after the break-in at the Homegrown Market, Ater was certain about one thing. On that night, Colton wasn't hungry. "Wherever he is, he's having a nice meal," he said.

Colton's defense attorney was asked on national television about the stunt at Ater's store months later, after Colton's arrest. The lawyer said Colton left the message as a joke, a spoof. "It was kind of like silly nineteen-year-old humor," the attorney said.

Beatrice von Tobel tells a joke about the Barefoot Bandit. Colton crashed two planes on her landing strip and stole one from one of the nearby hangars. She does some simple arithmetic to prove that Orcas Island ended up ahead. "He stole one," von Tobel said with a laugh, "and brought two."

CHAPTER FORTY

Two weeks after the chalk drawings at the Homegrown Market, the burglar alarm at Orcas Island Hardware was triggered early in the morning. The alarm quickly drew police and media attention back to this small island town that final day of February.

Someone broke a second-story window. Some people believe the person climbed onto a balcony and tried to bust in. Other people believe Colton just threw a rock through the window to trigger the alarm and watch the response. Nothing was taken, but the incident pointed to one primary suspect.

"Investigators believe the initial scene evidence suggests Colton Harris-Moore to be the prime person of interest," Sheriff Bill Cumming said. Police used a helicopter to search and a police dog was called in from the mainland. An extensive search of the area didn't lead to an arrest. Once again, Colton slipped away.

The next search for Colton was not in town. Instead, the search this time, two weeks after the last, was focused on the flanks of Turtleback Mountain, the aptly named landmark that fills much of the western portion of the island.

It was just after 1:15 a.m. on March 18 when a homeowner saw a tall, lanky teenager trying to break in. The man immediately suspected Colton. Police were called. The search was on again.

That morning, police from around the region raced to Anacortes to catch a ferry to Orcas and join in the manhunt for Colton. He'd been spotted in the densely wooded northwest corner of the island. Even with sirens blaring and emergency lights flashing, the trip to Orcas still involved a ferry ride. It took several hours for the additional police resources to join the search effort.

"He's believed to be in a very isolated and very rugged area on the west side of the island where only a few homes are located," Cumming said.

Police dogs and teams of manhunters joined in the effort. Heavily armed police went door-to-door looking for their suspect. Special agents with the FBI joined in. A U.S. Customs helicopter searched the area from above, including the mostly uninhabited western bluffs.

Colton's imminent capture seemed likely. Seattle-based reporters caught rides on helicopters to join the action. It seemed as though the end was near. But by late afternoon, the cops again had to throw in the towel. Colton wasn't going to be cornered, not this time.

Cumming said he'd keep the pressure up for a few days.

I asked him, that day in March, what if he caught Colton? What if he could put a quick end to the drama and nonsense?

"Wouldn't that be wonderful," the sheriff said.

CHAPTER FORTY-ONE

March 22, 2010, was Colton's nineteenth birthday. It came and went with no fanfare. No celebration. There was no massive manhunt. Probably no cake, either.

Police suspect Colton probably was huddling under a poncho in the woods, nibbling on stolen granola bars or chips. He could have been sleeping on a couch in an empty vacation home, or surfing porn.

Pam Kohler often called me to ask if I'd heard any news. One time she called to report a visit from FBI agents. She wanted to know if I could verify their story.

The agents told her a boat had gone missing from Orcas Island and was found afloat with no skipper. They suggested that Colton had fallen overboard and was missing.

Kohler was furious that the cops would scare a mother. The FBI wouldn't confirm the visit, or even the extent of their involvement in the case. They could have secured a court-approved warrant to wiretap Kohler's phone lines, but the paperwork has not been unsealed.

It's entirely conceivable the feds were working Kohler, playing games with her the way her son was playing games with them. She admitted her son called her. If she had information to provide the government, agents likely wanted her to confess what she knew. It's hard to know if they really concocted a story about a possible drowning, but police can turn up the pressure during interviews.

Colton's body didn't turn up as bait for the killer whales of the Salish Sea, of course. He was still hiding, still breaking into vacation homes, still plotting his next move.

Police tried a variety of tactics to catch Colton in addition to interviewing Kohler. They deployed specially trained man trackers. They hid motion sensors in empty homes on Camano Island. They used sophisticated helicopters, patrolled the waters off Orcas Island with Coast Guard cutters and tried through communication with other police forces to get one step ahead of the fugitive.

CHAPTER FORTY-TWO

Colton was on the move.

He'd recently taken a small boat from Cattle Point on San Juan Island and beached it about 10,000 feet away near Shark Reef on Lopez Island. How Colton managed to get from Orcas to San Juan Island isn't clear.

Bill Cumming, the San Juan County sheriff, confirmed that Colton was a suspect in the boat theft. "He left a lot of victims in his wake and I think his behavior certainly needs to be considered dangerous and getting more dangerous."

Locals call Lopez the friendly island. It's a quiet, rural place, a favorite among the San Juan Islands for cyclists, thanks to the rolling hills and lack of traffic. Rumors were reported that Colton slept during the day and roamed around at night, when people would be less likely to recognize the tall, skinny teenager. Others said he simply slipped a hoodie sweatshirt over his head and rode a stolen bicycle from place to place.

There were roadblocks set up on Lopez. Locals told me that police checked the trunks of cars and searched through yards, fields and sheds. They couldn't find Colton.

The warnings didn't worry Bill Moody, a Lopez Island builder whose home is not far from Shark Reef, the county park where Colton reportedly landed.

I met Moody on a beautiful summer afternoon after Colton's

capture. He was chatting with friends on the ferry from Lopez to San Juan Island and telling them the story of the Barefoot Bandit.

Moody told me he gladly would have invited Colton to join him and his friends for a few beers or to hang out in the hot tub. His opinion of Colton hadn't changed a few months later, after his capture, when I reached Moody at his home.

"I supported his mind, his brilliance to outsmart our intelligence of tracking people," he said. "Not too many people in our society walk on the edge like he was doing."

Moody said Colton easily could have marched by his property, where the doors often are left unlocked.

"He could have walked in and had a snack," Moody said. "If I'd known who he was, having to stay away from the law, and the law wouldn't like to hear this, I would have gladly fed the guy."

Moody is in his mid-fifties. He has an easy laugh and a mellow vibe. Moody said it would be a kick to have Colton over for dinner.

"It would be fun just to be in his presence and feel the energy that he vibrates around," Moody said.

If he had a message for Colton, it would be this: "Boy, you got a lot of balls to grab an airplane and fly it to the Bahamas. I mean, wow."

The United States can go all over the world, fighting wars, dropping bombs and hunting international terrorists, the builder said, but "how come they couldn't find one of our people on an island? The guy was sharp to be able to outrun the hounds."

Too few people have the survival instinct Colton demonstrated. For that, Colton deserved to be admired, Moody said.

Somehow, Colton had found a way to fend for himself. "That's what turns me on about him." And the builder wasn't the sole islander with this belief. "There are other people out there that would be right there on the wagon with me. I know I'm not alone."

After midnight on May 14, Colton walked quickly down the dock. It was 1:40 a.m. at Spencer's Landing Marina. He likely scoped out the small, private moorage at the very northern tip of Lopez Island. He didn't go unnoticed. A surveillance camera was filming and caught his image, albeit grainy and pixilated.

"The pictures show a young man, which the sheriff's department believes is Colton Harris-Moore, walking along a dock," Sheriff Bill Cumming said in a statement issued several days later along with the photos.

The *Stela Maris*, a sport fishing boat, soon was reported missing. The U.S. Coast Guard found the boat, adrift off the southern tip of Camano Island.

At the helm, Colton would have had the choice to skirt the western edge of Whidbey Island, past Keystone Harbor, before turning north into Possession Sound. An alternate route would have taken him through narrow and deep Deception Pass, through Skagit Bay and then south between Whidbey Island to the west and Camano Island to the east. Deception Pass is a tricky passage to navigate, even for a seasoned mariner. The narrow waterway doesn't leave much room for error.

Marine global positioning systems and radar are similar to the aeronautics equipment Colton already knew how to operate. The electronics on the *Stela Maris* probably were relatively user-friendly and easy to use. Most sport fishing boats are equipped with this kind of navigation technology. Colton would have passed lovely scenery along the way. He could have gazed out at the view of twinkling lights dancing off the cool waters. There may have been some fishermen on the water that night, or early-season recreational boaters, but for the most part Colton would have been surrounded by quiet. Whether at sea or land or in the skies, Colton was alone.

Coast Guard officials found the *Stela Maris* adrift off Gedney Island, a small island getaway in Tulalip Bay almost equidistant between Whidbey and Camano. It seemed obvious to assume that Colton was headed home.

The Island County Sheriff's Office tried to downplay the rumors.

"I know there is much speculation regarding possible Colton Harris-Moore involvement in this incident, but frankly it is just speculation on everyone's part at this time," Undersheriff Kelly Mauck said.

That didn't stop rumors from flying. At the Elger Bay Grocery customers shared concerns that the island's notorious son had returned. I spoke to Josh Flickner, the store's manager and the president of the Camano Island Chamber of Commerce. As Colton's infamy grew, Flickner became the de facto island spokesman, appearing on national news programs.

"It would seem very odd that it would not be Colton," Flickner said that day. Who else would steal a boat from the San Juan Islands only to ditch it off Camano Island's coast? Colton's likely return spurred Flickner to boost security at the store and at his home to protect his family.

"I won't be the only Camano Island resident that makes sure his gun is loaded tonight," Flickner said.

Colton appeared to be gone from the San Juan Islands. It looked as if he was headed home. Still, the cops on the San Juan Islands weren't ready to let down their guard. Sheriff Cumming said he wasn't going to take any chances. "There's no reason to believe he won't be coming back," he said. "Either way, we are cognizant of the fact he's been here twice and committed crimes."

Detectives never did pinpoint exactly where Colton made landfall in Island County. A dinghy from the south end of Camano was found across the water on Whidbey Island. Whether Colton actually used the dinghy or the small boat simply cut loose and drifted west is not known. Colton may have beached the *Stela Maris* on Whidbey or Camano and pushed her back afloat.

Although they couldn't pinpoint whether his landfall was on Whidbey or Camano, officials did determine that he'd left Whidbey Island. The clue came a couple of days later.

While taking his dog for a morning walk, a man on the Kitsap Peninsula, clear across Puget Sound west of Whidbey Island, found a powerboat hard aground on the beach.

When sheriff's deputies investigated, the 2002 Maxum powerboat was a mess. The ignition on the 27-foot boat had been ripped out and the interior was ransacked. Deputies got in touch with the boat's owner back on the southern end of Whidbey Island. The boat was found on May 24 but the owner wasn't sure how long it had been gone from the dock, likely several days.

The incident, like many connected to Colton, frustrated the local cops. There was little evidence left behind.

"I would say it's an open-ended answer," Kitsap County sheriff's spokesman Scott Wilson told a local television station. "We did not find any evidence on the boat that might indicate who the perpetrator might be."

There may not have been physical evidence, but there was circumstantial evidence that pointed to Colton. A new pattern rapidly was emerging of stealing boats and cars. The trip from Whidbey Island to the Kitsap Peninsula across the sound would be Colton's last in Puget Sound for years. He wasn't through stealing boats, though.

CHAPTER FORTY-THREE

The bounty hunters arrived at the school gymnasium in slick black cars, the windows tinted dark. They wore black clothes. The men's height and weight were as impressive as their determination.

The cops, the FBI, Homeland Security and the U.S. Coast Guard couldn't catch Colton. It was time for the bounty hunters to join the hunt.

"If he doesn't want to come forward, we need to find him," Mike Rocha told more than two hundred people at a hastily called community meeting at the Elger Bay Elementary School gymnasium on June 1.

Rocha has thick forearms and bulging biceps. His hair is closely cropped. He wears black polo shirts that fit taut across his chest. The announcement that Rocha, a bail-bond enforcement agent, had joined in the hunt for Colton came a few days earlier. It was a surprise because, although Colton was wanted, no bail-bond agent had posted a bond ensuring his return.

Typically, bonding agents are called in after someone is booked into jail. The legal system operates under the assumption that everyone is innocent until proven guilty. Courts err on the side of releasing prisoners unless there's a risk they will not return for court proceedings or that they are so violent and unpredictable they are a danger to the community. To make sure people show up and participate in the process, judges set bond. The dollar amount can range from a few hundred to millions of dollars for the most serious offenses.

Prisoners can either offer up cash bail for release or go to a bail-bond agency and pay a fee to a bail-bond agent, who in turn posts a bond with the court to obtain the prisoner's freedom. The bondsman's fee typically is about 10 percent of the bond amount. By default, a prisoner also has the choice to simply remain behind bars.

Once a deal is struck with the bail-bond agent, the bondsman offers the court a guarantee that the prisoner will show up for court. If the prisoner fails to show up, the bail-bond company sends an agent after the prisoner to help persuade him or her to appear.

Bondsmen I've talked to have always struggled to shake off the image created by the heavily blinged, mulleted and long-haired Duane "Dog" Chapman, the star of the hit television show *Dog the Bounty Hunter*. Local bail-bond agents say they're providing a community service as a for-profit arm of the criminal justice system that helps keep the process running smoothly. "We provide a great public service with no taxpayer dollars," Rocha said.

Bounty hunters have some advantages over police. They are not limited by jurisdictional boundaries; they don't need to worry about political ramifications of their actions or public funding. They also don't always have to play by the same rules as the cops. For example, when Dog the Bounty Hunter bursts into homes without search warrants, it's likely because the fugitive had signed a contract with the bail-bond agent waiving certain rights. Colton signed no such contract.

Recovery agents and bondsmen at times help police by having well-trained men and women with boots on the ground looking for bad guys, said John Gray, a former small-city police chief who now consults with police and teaches criminal justice at Northwestern University.

"They are great partners and can be another set of eyes and ears, but they are not substitutes for law enforcement," Gray said.

Gray was skeptical of someone outside of law enforcement being able to bring Colton to justice. Colton had been a fugitive for so long and was known to possess firearms.

"That probability makes this a matter for the professional peace officers to handle," he said. "They have the best professional practices, the resources and have a stake at continuing to earn the public's trust in keeping the community safe."

When Rocha announced he was going to make catching Colton his priority, serving as a liaison between victims and law enforcement, he was hardly met with enthusiasm by the Island County sheriff.

"I cannot promote or participate in this as a solution to the problem," Mark Brown said. "I will continue to share investigative information with the various police agencies involved in apprehending Colton Harris-Moore, but not to private interest groups, bounty hunters, etc."

I first met Rocha in Everett District Court's small video arraignment courtroom. This is the room where friends and relatives watch jailed prisoners make a first appearance in front of a judge via a closed-circuit video connection. Prisoners shuffle into a secure room at the jail where they are joined by a public defender, and sometimes a private defense attorney. The judge, prosecutor and visitors participate in the hearing on the first floor of the Snohomish County Courthouse. The brief hearing only determines if the state has probable cause to hold a defendant, and to allow the judge to set bail. I attended these hearings from time to time to report on high-profile arrests. Rocha attended for the opportunity to hand out his business card in hopes of drumming up business.

When Rocha told me he was offering to kick in $25,000 for a private reward fund and donate his own time to catch Colton, I asked him why.

"We have this problem that faces our society, and we want to help address it," Rocha said.

The idea to join the hunt, Rocha said, came after he was approached by a mysterious Seattle man who had started a blog called Catch the Barefoot Bandit. The blogger told me he was a writer and entrepreneur. He went by the pseudonym David Peters.

The blogger told me he'd spent time in the San Juan Islands and had many friends there. As legions of people were following Colton's exploits on fan pages, the blogger believed there needed to be another outlet to balance the public discourse.

"Any real community sentiments are being lost in the fanspeak," the blogger said. "The folk hero status is hyping and needs to be challenged." He quietly launched the site and then newspapers and other Web sites took notice.

Before the blogger launched his anti-Colton site, Internet searches would only return hits for Colton fan sites. "All the news seems to be glamorized," the blogger said. His friends were telling a contrary tale, one of victimization and violation. "They're tired of hearing his name," the blogger said. "Those [fan] sites seem to allow a destructive message to undermine citizens' higher standards and values."

The blogger flipped the equation. Where Sestak and others sought to support Colton, the blogger fought to bring him to justice. Whereas pro-Colton T-shirts and coffee mugs were sold from Sestak's site, the blogger launched his own line of merchandise spoofing Colton, mocking his inability to properly land an airplane and otherwise ridiculing the fugitive.

"I thought it would be good to poke fun," the blogger said.

Island County sheriff's detective Ed Wallace said he supported the idea of giving voice to Colton's victims. "From the beginning we've been against this whole hero mentality," Wallace said.

The detective stopped short of condoning any kind of vigilantism.

Within days, the blogger and Rocha connected. "Given the tremendous public outcry, it's natural that individuals and organizations would want to offer their expertise," the blogger said. Rocha seized the opportunity to capture the spotlight.

Despite increasing media interest in the story, investigators were keeping quiet. It was part of a measured strategy to downplay Colton's crimes. The FBI and others didn't want to discuss the case. Likely, authorities didn't want to feed the frenzy that could only have been encouraging Colton to continue. Evidence shows that Colton was using the Internet for a variety of purposes. He reportedly knew about the Facebook fan clubs and was reading the stories that were piling up about his exploits. Police found newspaper articles about the Barefoot Bandit at Colton's campsites.

Yet the silence on the part of law enforcement created a vacuum into which Rocha deftly stepped. For a few days he became the authoritative voice on catching Colton. That's how he managed to capture the attention of more than two hundred people on a drizzly early June evening on Camano Island.

The blogger, Peters, organized the meeting, but the Seattle man never showed up. Instead, Josh Flickner, the manager of the Elger Bay Grocery and the local Chamber of Commerce president, hosted the meeting.

Flickner said he would reopen a reward fund, first started in 2008, to help encourage people to bring information forward about Colton's comings and goings. Then Rocha took the microphone and outlined his plan. Rocha said he would apply his nearly thirty years of tracking bad guys to shake loose more information about Colton.

One way to entice Colton to come forward, Rocha said, was to offer the boy freedom while he waited for trial. Rocha was extending the opportunity for Colton to be released on bond at no cost.

"How many more experts do we need?" Camano Island resident Bec Thomas asked. Elizabeth Sounder, another resident, said Colton was on the run too long and it was time to catch him. The more people chasing him, the better chance for his capture, she said, adding, "He's caused a lot of heartache."

At the meeting, some people spoke compassionately about the teenager, urging him to surrender. One man, who refused to give his name to reporters, said he'd like to see Colton killed. The comment drew strong rebuke from the crowd.

All the fuss over Colton was having a ripple effect through the Camano Island economy. I spoke to J. P. DeBoer, a Realtor. "He's still at large and it's kind of a negative on the community." DeBoer didn't see a whole lot of value in Rocha's offers—he called the bounty hunter "a bit ridiculous"—but the topic of burglaries wasn't lost on the Realtor's potential customers. Security systems became a selling point for homes on the island.

I caught up with Rocha months after Colton's arrest. He stood by the efforts he made that spring. He and his colleagues offered up an experienced team to help flush Colton from his hiding spots. When Rocha's wife asked about the criticism mounted against him, Rocha said, "I don't give a shit."

Today people still recognize the bounty hunter and connect him to his part in the Colton saga. More frequently than not, people offer their support. "I think what we did was the right thing to do and I would do it again," Rocha said. "I feel good about what we did."

He admitted that much of what he said publicly at the time was part of the smoke-and-mirrors game played daily in his business. He knew it was unlikely he'd be able to post bond for Colton. It didn't matter so much what the truth was; what mattered was getting the suspect to surrender. What mattered to Rocha was getting Colton to start moving, to make him uncomfortable on his home turf, to force him out into the open. For accomplishing that, Rocha takes credit. "He became more and more vulnerable," Rocha said. "The eyes of the world were on him. It left him exposed."

CHAPTER FORTY-FOUR

A few days after the Camano Island community meeting, another person entered the media spotlight. Jim Johanson stepped forward with an offer for Colton. Johanson is a local attorney and former state legislator. He had recently run an unsuccessful campaign to become a county superior court judge.

The lawyer said he would represent Colton free of charge if the teen turned himself in. And he had added incentive for Colton. He had found an anonymous donor who put fifty thousand dollars on the block for Colton if he'd give up.

"It's just time for him to quit running," Johanson said at a press conference held in front of Rocha's Everett bail-bond office. Johanson spoke to Colton directly, via television news cameras: "Colton, I know you are tired. You need to trust someone."

The cash offer, made on a Thursday, came with a strict deadline. Colton had to make contact or turn himself in by the following Tuesday afternoon. The deadline came and went with no sign of Colton. "At this point the offer is going to be withdrawn," Johanson said.

I called Pam Kohler to see if she was interested in having Johanson represent her son, and to see what she had to say about the reward offer. "He's not interested in a lousy fifty thousand dollars for his freedom," Kohler said. She said she wasn't interested in Johanson. She didn't know the attorney and believed Colton would not want to work with him. Kohler said she would "do the best I can to talk him into going a different way" if Colton were to take Johanson up on his offer.

Kohler instead called a different lawyer, Seattle criminal defense attorney John Henry Browne. Browne agreed in principle to help the teen surrender safely to police. Browne is well known in the Pacific Northwest for defending a number of high-profile clients.

He reportedly eats raw vegetables for lunch, a diet that helps him to take on the most challenging cases. Browne represented Ted Bundy, the notorious serial killer, and Benjamin Ng, a man convicted in the 1983 Wah Mee Massacre that left thirteen people dead and remains Seattle's worst mass killing. Browne helped Ng avoid a death sentence. Browne reportedly has been through four marriages and practices meditation. As an assistant state attorney general, Browne fought for prison reforms and paved the way for Native Americans to be allowed to practice sweat lodge rituals behind bars. He enjoys a reputation as one of the best defense attorneys in the region.

When I first contacted Browne, he told me Kohler had called him at 11 p.m. one night to see if he might be interested in her son's case. "The answer is: 'Yeah, that's what I do for a living,' " he said.

Lawyers often will step forward to help a wanted individual safely surrender, Browne said. He was careful to point out that he wasn't fishing for the opportunity to represent Colton. It is only appropriate for a client to come looking for the lawyer's help, not the other way around, the lawyer said. Browne said the decision to work for the notorious teenager would only be made once he and Colton had met and both agreed the relationship was solid. Browne later did take the case.

Browne, who stands nearly eye-to-eye with Colton, first met the now six-foot-five fugitive in an interview room at the federal courthouse in Seattle. After a brief hearing in front of a federal judge, Browne told a group of reporters that he wanted to go by a new name, "the Barefoot Lawyer."

CHAPTER FORTY-FIVE

In the middle of the night the team of bounty hunters set up surveillance at harbors, airports and other places Colton could be lurking. On several nights, the bounty hunters set out in a small boat to try to snare Colton.

Rocha invited me to go along, but I declined. I calculated the odds were good that I'd spend an evening being wet and cold, not catching a glimpse of Colton.

Richard Grover, seventy, hoped to have a different way of finding Colton. I met Grover at the community meeting on Camano Island a few weeks before and he'd been persistent in calling me, eager to share his story.

Grover, who often lives out of his car, said he developed a skill for tracking Colton and had been on the fugitive's tail for weeks, even months. Grover used an ancient practice known as dowsing. Dowsing involves holding a Y-shaped stick and allowing special senses to let the stick point to a source. The method is most often used to find water or underground metals. It's unusual but not unheard of for dowsers to track people.

Grover told me he spent forty years tracking Sasquatch using the dowsing techniques. "Nobody believes me," he said.

Grover believed he first caught a glimpse of Colton while the older man was camping on Orcas Island. "While turning around on a dead-end road, I spotted someone sitting motionless in the bushes next to my van. The thought came to me it could be Colton!" Grover wrote in a two-page typed memo he shared with me in early June 2010. (Deputies determined the person Grover saw was a resident walking in the woods, not the serial burglar.)

"I began to understand why he is doing this," Grover wrote, linking his own broken childhood to Colton's fragmented and tumultuous upbringing. "Even as a small child I began to pray that someday I may be able to be of use to humanity and make a difference," Grover wrote. "So to Colton I would like to send this message that I wish to become like a friend you never had or Dad you never had!"

Grover wrote that he believed Colton's resourcefulness could be put to good use. What would happen, Grover wondered, if Colton's energy could be channeled in the right direction. "I became in [a] strange sort of way a member in his fan club," Grover wrote. "Not one in support of his activities, but one who would like to see him look through the telescope from the opposite end and seek a better way to live, one where there is peace and love and understanding and great joy!"

When I caught up with Grover again, he told me he'd successfully tracked Colton to a horse barn on the northwest corner of Camano Island. "He's been quiet lately," Grover said. "He might be planning something else."

Colton was planning something else but not on Camano Island. By the time Grover and I talked, Colton was hundreds of miles away, headed east.

PART SIX
ROAD TRIP

CHAPTER FORTY-SIX

Colton already had been compared to Robin Hood. It wasn't until he slipped through the small community of Raymond, Washington, sometime during Memorial Day weekend that he actually gave money away.

As he sped by Vetters Animal Hospital along the main road that leads through this rural and remote part of southwest Washington, Colton decided to leave money and a message.

Colton stopped his stolen car and left one hundred dollars and a handwritten note at the vet clinic. It was either May 30 or May 31; police couldn't pinpoint the date.

"Drove by, had some extra cash. Please use this cash for the care of animals," Colton wrote. He signed the letter: "Colton Harris-Moore, aka, the Barefoot Bandit." Police in Raymond collected the note and sent it to the state crime laboratory, where it was authenticated. The money was seized as evidence.

Colton's mom and some of his childhood friends said he had a love for animals, especially Melanie, his pet beagle mix. It didn't matter what good intentions Colton had for the cash; it wasn't his to give away, Raymond police chief Ken Boyes said. The fugitive was unemployed and the money likely was stolen. "He probably hasn't filed a tax return," the police chief said. The whole thing wasn't intended as a charitable display, Boyes said. It was an attempt to mock police. Colton was saying, "Here I am. Catch me if you can," the chief believed.

Pam Kohler was incensed when I called her. She said Colton did have a job and had earned money. She told me she was proud to learn that Colton had tried to make a donation to help animals.

"If Colt wanted a hundred bucks to go to them, I'll send them a hundred bucks," she said. The vet clinic confirmed that Kohler followed through on her promise.

Chief Boyes said he didn't know of any law Colton had violated in his jurisdiction, but he knew enough of the tale of the Barefoot Bandit to say this: "The guy is dangerous and needs to be apprehended."

Fugitives either run away or run toward something, said Mike Rocha, the bounty hunter. Colton was continuing to move. "He was running away," Rocha said. "There was nothing to run toward."

CHAPTER FORTY-SEVEN

The Columbia Bar is one of the most notorious maritime graveyards on the Pacific Coast. This is where the mighty Columbia River spews into the Pacific Ocean, causing rip-tides and massive waves. Before modern navigational aids were put in place and highly paid bar pilots were commissioned to guide ships across the bar, the region was known as the Graveyard of the Pacific. The head of land that stretches out to meet the bar from the north is appropriately named Cape Disappointment. It's home to a world-renowned life-boat school and has one of the busiest U.S. Coast Guard stations in the country.

Had Colton veered west out of the Ilwaco marina on the morning of June 1, 2010, in the *Fat Cat*, a stolen $450,000 motorboat, he would have had to navigate the tricky and often deadly waters of the Columbia Bar. Instead, he directed the *Fat Cat* southeast, aiming toward the southern end of the Astoria-Megler Bridge, the three-quarters of a mile cantilever truss-span that connects Washington and Oregon via Highway 101.

He landed at a commercial marina in the small town of Warrenton, a working-class community that exists in the shadow of its better-known neighbor, the tourist landmark of Astoria. Colton carefully secured the stolen 34-foot Ocean Sport powerboat and took off. An alert harbormaster in Warrenton called police after he found the *Fat Cat*. The pleasure boat was out of place among the hulking fishing vessels, Warrenton police chief Matthew Workman said.

The *Fat Cat*'s discovery fit a pattern of connected crimes that would eventually link to similar crimes in a spree that extended thousands of miles across nine states. In Warrenton, the trail led from the marina about three miles away to the Astoria Regional Airport. Investigators knew almost immediately they were looking for just one suspect in the string of crimes. "We have a very quiet, low-crime community," Workman told me. "It stands to reason they would be related."

At first officials couldn't definitely pin the evidence on Colton. But Colton left behind a fingerprint on the boat. An Oregon crime laboratory later linked the evidence to the Camano Island teen. (In the flurry of Colton news that was being generated at the time, initial reports quoted Workman saying that officials had identified Colton's footprints. Skeptical, I contacted Workman to determine if the previous media report was wrong. He confirmed it was Colton's fingerprint, not footprints, that were analyzed and matched.)

At the airport, Colton tried to pry open the doors of a Cessna, the same make of plane he'd flown in two previous joyrides. Thwarted, Colton broke into the Hertz rental car office at the airport and grabbed the keys to a 2010 Dodge Journey. Unfortunately for the cops, the rental car office was not equipped with security cameras.

"We were kind of out of luck on the surveillance images," Workman said.

Back in Island County, Detective Ed Wallace and his partner, Mark Plumberg, had put together Colton's M.O. and were trying to catch up with him. It was clear Colton was leaving a trail of stolen boats and vehicles behind.

Wallace had quietly observed the June 1 Camano Island meeting with Rocha. The detective later told me he had to bite his lip the whole evening. Wallace already knew that Colton was hundreds of miles away. The bounty hunter's effort may have persuaded Colton not to return to Camano Island, but Colton appears to have left on his own.

Officials tried to chart out a course of small regional airports where Colton might be headed. The investigators hoped Colton would make a mistake. "The farther he stretched from his home base, the greater chance of his being caught," Wallace said.

The trail picked up when a farmer near Dayton, Oregon, a rural community about an hour south of Portland, noticed the shiny new sport utility vehicle parked near his property. He didn't think much about it at first. Then, when the truck was still parked there the next day, he realized it just wasn't right. He called the cops. The stolen SUV from the Hertz car rental in Warrenton was recovered.

CHAPTER FORTY-EIGHT

Things weren't right in Graham Goad's office at the McMinnville Municipal Airport. Hot dogs were disappearing from the office refrigerator. The computer had been reset. The Internet connection unplugged.

McMinnville sits near the center of Oregon's Willamette Valley, a region known for growing world-class pinot noir grapes. It also has links to aviation history. In 1950, the local paper published photos of UFOs but the more lasting connection is the Evergreen Aviation Museum, home of Howard Hughes' famous *Spruce Goose*, the hulking seaplane that flew only once.

Colton didn't stay long enough to go on wine tastings or visit the exhibits at the museum.

Goad opened his refrigerator on two different occasions to discover missing food. The first time was on a Monday, then again on a Wednesday.

News of the Barefoot Bandit had spread among the aviation community and Goad knew Colton's story. He hadn't heard that Colton was in Oregon, but learned of the Bandit's trip south when Goad's brother called from Everett.

Dayton, the town where the stolen Dodge from Warrenton was recovered, is about three miles from McMinnville. It would have taken Colton less than an hour to walk the distance to the airport.

Goad walked across the tarmac to the flight school for a morning cup of coffee. He learned food was missing from there, too. "Maybe it's the Barefoot Bandit," he wondered. A little while later, the woman at the flight school called Goad to report that a Cadillac Escalade was missing.

The flight school also serves as the airport's FBO, or fixed base operator, which is kind of like the harbormaster of an airport. A family had flown into McMinnville, rented the Caddy from Enterprise Rent-A-Car, then returned it at the FBO, leaving the keys with the manager, who in turn would give the vehicle back to the rental car business. "The following day the car was recovered at the Ontario airport," Goad said. Ontario is hundreds of miles away, clear across Oregon on the Idaho border.

In hindsight, Goad's near encounter was little more than a skipping stone in Colton's journey east.

I called Goad again after Colton's arrest in the Bahamas. "I was impressed that he made it that far in an airplane having as little flight training, or no formal flight training," Goad said. "The kid's smart, not stupid—on the other hand, he is stupid."

Goad, who is himself a pilot and flight instructor, never would let an inexperienced pilot fly on his own. Learning to fly takes hours of training, both on the ground and with an instructor in the air. "I sure as heck wouldn't let them go out after a few hours," he said.

Colton had guts and was lucky, Goad said.

As for Colton's time in McMinnville, Goad summed it up this way: "He's hungry and likes to travel."

CHAPTER FORTY-NINE

Like Hansel and Gretel's bread crumbs, stolen cars began to be recovered by police in a trail that headed east from central Oregon. Cops in Ontario, Oregon, on the border with Idaho, found the stolen Escalade at the city's small airport. An airport hangar in Ontario was broken into and a pilot's truck was stolen. That truck was found between Ontario and Boise, Idaho.

The towns and cities lined up like a tour route through the West and Midwest. Police in Cody, Wyoming, found Colton's DNA in a vehicle stolen on June 13. That vehicle was recovered the next day 180 miles away in Buffalo, Wyoming. Colton's trail next picked up at a small airport in Spearfish, South Dakota. From Spearfish, the trail continued east about four hundred miles to Yankton, South Dakota.

Colton was never very good at concealing evidence at his crime scenes. Even though he tried using bleach in one burglary, and pouring oil in the cockpit of Pat Gardiner's Cessna, the cops typically found hard evidence in his wake. They found fingerprints, DNA on water bottles, clipped hair and droplets of blood.

John Gray, former police chief and now law enforcement consultant, told me that catching Colton was only a piece of the law enforcement equation.

"Months after he is in custody, the quality of the physical

evidence that is collected and preserved, the willingness of citizen witnesses to step up and participate in the justice system, and the scrutiny of what the police did will determine what will eventually happen with Mr. Harris-Moore," Gray said. "Apprehension is only one piece of this work."

It was around 3 a.m. and Kelly Kneifl's family was exhausted from a day of traveling. The final leg, a three-hour drive from the airport in Omaha to their recently purchased home in Yankton, South Dakota, was over.

Kelly Kneifl could have routed the family's journey to visit relatives back east through the small airport that is practically next door to their home. But paying for a family of six to travel is expensive. It was much cheaper to book the flights to Pennsylvania out of the larger commercial airport in Omaha.

By the time he rolled up the driveway early the morning of June 18, Kelly Kneifl was the only one awake in the SUV. He gently nudged his wife from her sleep.

Kneifl pulled into the garage, but something wasn't quite right. "We noticed the door wasn't quite how we left it," he said. His wife was carrying the youngest child, a five-year-old girl, when she noticed a door ajar across the entranceway.

"She saw a hand grab that door and slam it shut," he said. She hollered for help.

The scene played out like an action movie. Kneifl sprang into action and ran into the house. He confronted a tall, naked, boyish young man running through the home. Kneifl gave chase. The intruder vaulted down the basement stairs. "I was screaming at the top of my voice," Kneifl said. At the time, Kneifl believed the naked man was a neighborhood kid. He figured there must be a naked woman nearby, too.

As Kneifl started to descend the basement steps, he saw a

red laser beam land on his torso. It was aimed at his chest. "He said, 'Stop, I've got a gun. I'll shoot,'" Kneifl remembers. Not wanting to be shot, Kneifl backed out of the house, gathered up his family in the SUV and drove quickly to a neighbor's driveway to call the cops. His wife frantically called 911. She told dispatchers there was an armed man in her home.

"I don't know if it was a [laser] pointer or a gun," Kneifl said. "I had no idea. I decided I'm just going to get out." Yankton police arrived within minutes, but kept their sirens off. Three days earlier there had been a break-in at the airport, less than a mile from Kneifl's home. The cops had their suspicions that Colton was lurking nearby. Word of the Barefoot Bandit was spreading among law enforcement.

As the cops started to investigate, Kneifl sent his wife and the four children, ages five, eight, twelve and fifteen, to a hotel to get some sleep. He stayed behind and, while SWAT teams were mustered, helped the police understand the layout of the home. About an hour after Kneifl's encounter with a naked Colton, heavily armed police entered the home. Colton was gone.

He left behind a mess, and evidence of his two- or three-day stay. Kneifl believes he used one of his razors to trim his hair. There was about an inch of clippings on the floor. Colton slept in Kneifl's son's bedroom, watched television and helped himself to food. Colton left a pizza in the oven and a plate of chicken nuggets on the counter. He had raided the refrigerator, helping himself to deli meats and Jell-O pudding cups. "Typical kid stuff, you know," Kneifl said.

It looked as though Colton had taken care of other necessities, too. He was almost through washing his clothes. Before Colton slipped out a back window, he'd grabbed his laundry, breaking the washing machine's lid and leaving behind a pair of clean underwear.

Investigators spent about four hours combing for evidence—DNA from utensils, samples of hair—before clearing the house around 7 a.m., Kneifl said. For the next several nights, his kids were startled by noises in the night. They gathered mattresses in their parents' room to sleep. "It was tough for a while," he said.

Throughout the ordeal, Kneifl worked hard to keep his emotions at bay. Someone in the family had to stay strong, he said. For days, he fielded interview requests from reporters all over the country eager to hear about his encounter with the Barefoot Bandit. He reenacted his encounter for CBS News cameras.

Now that the media storm had subsided, Kneifl said he's still angry about the burglary at his home, but feels better knowing he was randomly targeted. "I was upset that my house was violated," he said.

Yankton assistant police chief Jerry Hisek told me his department didn't take any chances as they hunted for Colton. The cops feared Colton was armed. Investigators also knew of Colton's habit of running. The police went house to house, making sure Colton hadn't ducked inside to hide. By dawn, they gave up. Colton had escaped.

As news spread that Colton had popped up on the map, reporters from around the country besieged Hisek. The policeman told the *Yankton Press-Dakotan* he was fielding twenty calls a day. Hisek said he'd never in more than three decades of law enforcement experienced anything like the frenzy over the Barefoot Bandit. "It was kind of hectic," Hisek said. "I don't want to downplay what took place here, but it was because of who he was."

CHAPTER FIFTY

The next stop on Colton's tour of small airports across the west was the Karl Stefan Memorial Airport, a small public airport just south of Norfolk, Nebraska. The field is named for a former newspaper editor and longtime congressman.

The call that something was amiss came in late morning. The first cop showed up after 11 a.m. on June 19. Someone had tried to pry open the doors using some kind of tool. The lone officer sent to investigate looked around, along with airport staff. They couldn't tell for sure if anyone had been able to get in.

Later they learned that Colton had been able to break in. Although he didn't succeed in stealing a plane, they determined that he must have been cold. Days later in Ottumwa, Iowa, police found a blue zip-up sweatshirt with tan embroidery: "Norfolk Airport" was stitched onto the front along with a picture of an airplane. Terri Wachter, the airport manager, told police the forty-dollar sweatshirt was missing from the Karl Stefan Memorial Airport office. No one had noticed it missing at first for a simple reason. It was too hot out; the sweatshirt wasn't being used.

The same cop who went to the Karl Stefan Airport the previous day to investigate a burglary was sent to Ta Ha Zouka Park. The park is 180 acres of pristine country along the Elkhorn River. The park dates back to the Great Depression and was built under funding by the Works Progress Administration. A Norfolk police officer was sent to investigate an abandoned Toyota Sequoia with South Dakota plates. He found the vehicle at 7:19 a.m. on June 20, almost exactly twenty-four hours after it was reported stolen to police.

When police in Norfolk caught up with their colleagues in Yankton, where Colton had terrified the Kneifl family, investigators learned all about Colton Harris-Moore, the Barefoot Bandit. By then, Yankton police had talked to the FBI and cops back in Washington and Oregon. Although Colton was making headlines nationally and being featured in glossy magazines, there were plenty of police officers in America who were not aware of him or his M.O. Police were sharing top-line information about Colton as widely as they could. Still, even though information about Colton's M.O. was being shared, the cops couldn't quite catch up with him.

Back at the Karl Stefan Memorial Airport, it became clear that Colton had been able to break into the office and at least one of the hangars. Even though he left cash and other valuables undisturbed, he still tried to cover his tracks. Colton targeted the surveillance system and attempted to break it.

Then he went to a hangar and decided to try to get into Darwin Puls' plane. Colton struggled to get the right-side cockpit door open, but it was locked. He instead went around to the other side of the plane. From there he hoped he could reach his long arm inside and open a door. But his arm wasn't long enough. He looked around for something he could use to unlock the cabin door.

"The working theory is the suspect then unscrewed a broom head off a broom handle and stuck the broom handle through the small window," Norfolk police detective Ben McBride wrote in court papers. "The suspect was unsuccessful."

Puls discovered the attempted break-in when he returned to the hangar to fly the plane back to Georgia. He'd been visiting Nebraska to attend a family wedding. I caught up with him months later, after he'd just landed his plane in South Dakota. I asked him what he thought about Colton.

"I would sure like to spend three or four minutes in a dark room with him," Puls told me. Puls definitely is not a member of the Colton Harris-Moore Fan Club.

Puls said he had parked his Moony M20J and locked the four-seater plane in what he believed was a secure hangar. It's not clear why Colton tried to get into Puls' plane, but it could be that Puls' aircraft was equipped with a Garmin G500 computer, a GPS similar to what Colton already knew how to operate. While Colton managed to break the fifteen-dollar door lock, he couldn't get into the plane. "Fortunately he gave up on it," Puls said.

The episode delayed Puls about two and a half hours while he waited for detectives to investigate and collect evidence. "The hardest thing about the whole deal was cleaning the fingerprint stuff off the wing," he said.

Puls saved his anger for Colton's mom and what he called the "liberal bullshit thinking" that allowed Kohler to praise her son's criminal exploits in the national media. Colton would have been a productive citizen had he been properly brought up, the pilot said. "The whole thing could have been avoided if his mother had beat the shit out of him," Puls said. "Little bulls need to be trained and apparently he never got trained."

The pilot didn't remain on the phone long enough for me

to explain that Colton did get the "shit" beaten out of him, and that likely contributed to his behavior.

Colton couldn't break into Puls' plane and he wasn't successful at disabling the video surveillance. A technician was able to fix the hard drive of the surveillance system and found images. At four minutes before 3 a.m. on June 19, a tall, lanky suspect with dark hair could be seen going into the airport services building. As he walked through a door, he grabbed the doorframe, leaving fingerprints. The suspect also left fingerprints on Puls' plane and on the broom handle. When detectives in Washington and in Nebraska reviewed the footage and compared it to other images of Colton, they could come to only one conclusion. "It appears the suspect is likely Colton Harris-Moore," McBride wrote in a report.

During the investigation, the police were told that a gray 2008 Cadillac Escalade was missing from the Norfolk airport.

Now police across five states were actively sharing information. By June 23, local cops in Nebraska reached FBI special agent Linwood "Chip" Smith in Seattle. Smith explained that the feds had case files on Colton and were monitoring his movements. Colton was on the move. It would be another few weeks before the FBI would unseal a federal criminal complaint filed in December 2009 against Colton.

CHAPTER FIFTY-ONE

Colton made his way next to Pella, Iowa, about 275 miles east of Norfolk. Police knew Colton was there because the Escalade, stolen in Norfolk, was recovered in Pella on June 21. That's the same day a burglary was reported at Classic Aviation in Pella. A van and cash were missing, police said.

The next day, cops found the stolen van in Ottumwa, Iowa, about a half-hour drive east toward Illinois. There, Colton tried to break into at least one airplane before he gave up. Sometime between 7 p.m. on June 22 and 4:25 p.m. the next day, Colton allegedly stole a Frito-Lay delivery truck. He damaged the truck and helped himself to several bags of the snack food. Colton left behind more than crumbs. Investigators found several fingerprints. There also was a break-in at a Mexican restaurant and then the trail led to the city's water and hydro facility. That's where police believe Colton stole a white Chevrolet HHR, a crossover sport utility vehicle with rounded edges. Colton seemed to prefer luxury SUVs, but he was in a bind and had to keep moving.

Ottumwa's Chevy HHR was found by 8 a.m. on June 24. A side window was smashed out and the car was stuck in the mud in a creek bed.

The spring weather had been unforgiving with rains and

floods. The waters filled the Mississippi River and the tributaries that run into the big river. If Colton had been more familiar with the area, he probably could have avoided getting the car stuck. He would have known the route he chose was impassable.

But Colton was far from home. He didn't have a plan. He was just heading east to the next airport, hoping for a chance, an opportunistic break to flee. The mud caught him. He tried, unsuccessfully, to free his stolen ride.

"Somebody used the shovel out of the car to dig the car out," chief deputy Scott Bentzinger said. "But he was unsuccessful."

The Chevy was found about a hundred miles east of Ottumwa in an unincorporated part of Dallas City, Illinois, just across the Mississippi.

Pam Kohler told me she believed Colton was headed to visit mysterious friends of his on the East Coast. She didn't know who they were or where they lived. "I know he had people he knows on the East Coast, or at least that's what he told me," she said. She said she hadn't spoken to Colton in months.

At the time she reiterated her belief that there were copycat criminals at work and that Colton couldn't be responsible for every crime along a crime trail that now stretched thousands of miles. And she had another comment: "He ought to steal a plane and get the hell out of the States."

That's exactly what Colton planned to do.

Meanwhile, Harley Davidson Ironwing was busted for shoplifting string cheese. Harley was hungry. He told the cops he hadn't eaten in three days.

Harley was back in his hometown of Stanwood on that late June day. A grocery store employee spotted him sneaking the snack food and gave chase. A commotion followed outside and a sheriff's deputy joined the ruckus. Harley darted in a different direction and both the fleeing suspect and the cop barreled into an elderly couple, knocking an eighty-four-year-old man to the ground.

Officials feared the older man had broken a shoulder, but he was checked out, and it was determined that he was shaken up but otherwise fine. The string cheese theft earned Harley another year and a half behind bars.

About six months before the shoplifting incident, Harley told me he was trying to turn the corner, to do right and stop doing wrong. "I basically just blew away my whole childhood," he said. "I'm twenty years old now. I got to grow up."

PART SEVEN

ESCAPE TO PARADISE

CHAPTER FIFTY-TWO

The police in Bloomington were expecting Colton. There was extra security at the airport. It didn't stop him. Colton broke into a secure airfield, into a locked hangar, and stole a fully fueled Cessna 400 Corvalis. The keys were in the ignition. Could it have been any easier?

Colton probably read the manual of the Garmin G1000 GPS in John Miller's plane. He carefully programmed in a destination: the Bahamas.

John Miller had stopped into his office on Independence Day. When his cell phone rang, interrupting him, he gazed at the caller ID, didn't recognize the number, and decided to let the call go into voice mail.

Miller, who works for a beer distributor, left his office and went to hit some balls at the driving range. He wanted to get in a bit of exercise. On the way, he listened to the message on his cell phone. He couldn't believe it.

"I immediately made the turn to the airport," Miller said.

The U.S. Coast Guard had picked up an emergency beacon from Miller's plane off the coast of the Bahamas. Did Miller know where his plane was? Miller believed he did know. His plane was in the locked hangar where he'd left it, right? No. If the plane's emergency transponder went off, the plane was gone. The message was from a Coast Guard official. They had his plane. "They don't make mistakes," Miller said.

Miller had just returned to Bloomington the day before. He was planning on making a short flight the following week. The plane was due for an oil change and he wanted to squeeze it in before his next trip. Miller called the FBO, the fixed base operator, to see if he could schedule the maintenance. The FBO manager told Miller he could get the work done, no problem. Miller left the keys to his $650,000 airplane in the ignition, trusting the FBO manager.

The Cessna 400 Corvalis is a sleek, gorgeous single-engine plane. It's the fastest single-engine plane on the market and can reach speeds of about 240 miles per hour. "That's the Porsche of the single-engine airplanes," said Jan Sawyer, a flight instructor in Memphis, Tennessee. "It's the fastest fixed-gear aircraft." Plus, compared to other comparable planes, the Corvalis is fuel-efficient.

The interior has leather. It has air-conditioning. The plane was outfitted with special GPS electronics including a Wide Area Augmentation System, or WAAS. The newest in flight technologies, WAAS allows pilots to descend and land on a gentle slope, as opposed to a tiered system. "It's a great invention," Miller said.

When the FBO came to fetch Miller's plane, he had to tow it clear across the airfield from Miller's hangar to the maintenance area. "If the kid was watching the field, he would have seen the plane . . . moved," Miller said.

And that's what Miller believed happened. After the oil was changed, Miller's plane was towed back to the hangar, where a crew started the engine to make sure it wasn't leaking oil. A fuel truck was called over and topped off the tanks. The plane was returned to the hangar and the keys left in the ignition.

Unlike other airplanes that use a key to turn on the starter and then a switch to start the engines, the Cessna 400 starts like a car. The pilot turns the key and the engine roars to life.

If Miller had known there was a fugitive in the area, he never would have told the FBO to leave the key. "He could have had the key placed elsewhere," Miller said. But it's too late for that. "It's water over the dam."

Colton crashed Miller's plane more than a thousand miles away, in a mangrove swamp a few miles off the coast of Great Abaco Island, knocking one of the wheels off the plane. News crews found barefoot prints in the mud nearby. Witnesses saw the plane circle a few times before it went down.

Colton didn't immediately run off. He stuck around the crash, pulled out the plane's seat cushions and napped under the fuselage. Then he clambered through the muck as he made his way ashore. One can only imagine how exhausted, elated and spent Colton must have been. The warm, salty water likely was refreshing, but Colton would have been hungry and thirsty. Hiking through the knee-deep muck was hard work. Producers for *48 Hours Mystery* tried to repeat the trek by foot but got so tired and dirty they opted instead to have a helicopter take them to the crash site.

Once ashore, Colton's first target in the Bahamas probably was Dwight Pinder's small gas station. Pinder told reporters his shop was burglarized the night after the plane crash. The thief took Gatorade and two small bags of potato chips. He left behind more food and drink, leading Pinder to believe that whoever broke into his small shop must have had to leave in a hurry.

Within hours of the reported plane crash, Bahamian officials started getting word of other burglaries. A home was broken into and a vehicle was stolen, officials said. As news of the plane crash spread, federal agents in the United States turned up the heat.

If Mike Rocha and his team of bounty hunters took credit for flushing Colton from his home turf, Colton's international flight can be credited for shaking loose the FBI. Time and again, the FBI said they considered Colton "a backyard nuisance," a burglar and thief best left to the worries of local law enforcement. The flight to the Bahamas changed that.

"We want to get him," FBI Special Agent Steven Dean said the Tuesday after the plane crash. "He's turned from a regional nuisance into an international problem." Dean added, "If that is in fact him." FBI wanted posters featuring three photos of Colton were distributed. The U.S. government added a $10,000 reward for information leading to the fugitive's arrest.

Officials also unsealed a secretly filed federal criminal complaint against Colton. On December 11, 2009, Special Agent Linwood "Chip" Smith filed the five-page complaint in U.S. District Court in Seattle, alleging Colton was responsible for stealing the plane that crashed in the clear-cut near Granite Falls. Colton was charged by complaint with one count of interstate transportation of stolen property, a crime punishable by up to ten years in prison.

The criminal complaint began to set the stage for the broader case against Colton. For the first time, prosecutors linked Colton affirmatively to the plane theft from Bonners Ferry, Idaho. They accused Colton of stealing firearms from an airplane hangar in Creston, British Columbia, and connected him to more than five dozen other crimes. The government's estimate of the number of crimes Colton committed would increase rapidly as more paperwork was filed with the courts.

Another key detail about Colton's unique brand of criminal behavior was confirmed in the unsealed criminal complaint. Special Agent Smith noted Colton's reputation for running barefoot as a kid. He used that distinguishing factor to connect the teen to evidence found in Bonners Ferry and in Granite Falls. Investigators at both locations found barefoot prints "consistent with those left by Harris-Moore at other crime scenes."

The FBI confirmed what the nation already knew: Colton was the Barefoot Bandit.

Back in Bloomington, Miller couldn't believe his plane was gone. The Monroe County Airport had been on alert after police found a stolen car in a nearby church parking lot, Miller later learned. "Lo and behold, everyone else in the area knew," Miller said.

He'd never heard of Colton Harris-Moore or the Barefoot Bandit.

Surveillance video from the FBO at the Bloomington airport showed Miller's plane taxiing by the control tower early on the Fourth of July. Colton taxied to the end of runway 17, gunned the engines and lifted Miller's plane into the sky.

After takeoff, the plane's transponder already was preset to send out the correct signal. "He was squawking 1200," Miller said. The 1200 signal tells flight control managers the pilot is on his own and likely not monitoring air traffic frequencies. It's a virtual thumbs-up.

Air control operators may have seen Miller's plane flying by. They may have even worried because the plane could have been flying at the wrong altitude. But by squawking 1200, the air traffic operators wouldn't try to contact Miller's plane. Instead, they'd reach out to other pilots who were on their radios and tell those pilots to change direction or altitude, Miller said.

Miller believes Colton didn't touch the plane's two-way radio. "My guess is he didn't say a word to anybody" during the four-hour flight from the Midwest to the Bahamas, Miller said.

Colton would have enjoyed the ride. Miller's plane was a finely tuned, high-performance machine. Colton was cruising above the Southeast at more than 200 miles an hour. He wasn't just surviving; he was living large. The towns drifted by below him and Colton finally arrived at the Atlantic Coast. He glimpsed the coral blue waters of another ocean for the first time.

The plane veered slightly left and he bid the mainland good-bye as he made the 70-mile jump to the Bahamas. Colton made it out of the country.

Miller believes Colton flew until he ran out of gas. The teen pilot really didn't have to worry about much else, other than landing. It wouldn't have been that difficult for Colton to avoid flying through restricted airspace. In reality, there aren't many places that limit pilots. There are rules around commercial airports, but Miller's sophisticated GPS would have helped Colton steer clear. The same goes for Fort Knox or the Kennedy Space Station in Florida, the only other restricted areas in his potential path.

If Colton was tracking his route on the GPS, the electronic maps would have showed red areas to avoid. Colton could have easily steered away. "It'd be a piece of cake, if he understood restricted airspace, not to go near it," Miller said.

CHAPTER FIFTY-THREE

Pam Kohler, Colton's mother, was infuriated by the news. Not that Colton had flown one thousand miles. Not that he left the country and hadn't surrendered. No, Colton had it all wrong. He went to a country that had an extradition treaty with the United States and he flew in the wrong kind of plane, Kohler said.

"The further he gets from the U.S., the better . . . I'm glad he's able to enjoy beautiful islands," Kohler said. But there was a problem with the Bahamas. The long arm of U.S. law enforcement could still reach into the small island country. "They extradite," she said. "It doesn't help matters at all."

She also didn't like the news that Colton had flown in a Cessna 400. "Colt is not to be flying a single-engine plane. When I heard that, that just upset me," Kohler said. "The rules are he carries a parachute with him and takes two-engine planes."

Colton didn't follow his mom's rules. None of the airplanes he stole was two-engine, which perhaps worked to his benefit. Statistically, more people die in twin-engine planes than the single-engine variety, experts said. Typically if one motor on a twin-engine plane stops working, the second engine doesn't do much but "guides the plane to the crash site," one flying expert told me.

Still, Kohler was desperate to hear directly from Colton. "Tell him to call me," she said.

The Bahamians launched an effort to try to close down any escape routes Colton might discover.

"We have taken steps to neutralize the areas he may try to use to leave the island," said Hulan Hanna, an assistant superintendent of police.

Police on the island handed out FBI wanted posters featuring several photos of Colton. The poster was added to the FBI's Seattle Web site alongside other local most-wanted men, including arsonists and murderers. On the poster, the FBI warned that Colton could be armed.

Everyone suspected that Colton, a tall, lanky white man, would stand out in the Bahamas, where much of the population is black. But he wasn't the only visitor to the islands that week. It was Regatta Time, an annual sailing event that draws thousands of tourists. It's possible Colton could have blended in with the crowds.

Four days after the crash, officials believed they had Colton cornered on Abaco Island. At least seven burglaries were reported that week in a community where crime typically doesn't occur.

"If he stays on the island long enough, police will probably catch him," said Alistair McDonald, a restaurant owner whose business, the Curly Tails pub, was burglarized early Tuesday, with Colton the prime suspect.

It was an odd crime. McDonald said surveillance cameras captured a glimpse of the six-foot, five-inch serial burglar before the intruder turned the cameras toward the walls. The burglar didn't take anything.

McDonald said Colton's white skin wouldn't be the only

reason he'd stand out. On the small islands, people know one another. "It's hard to blend in if you're not from here," he said.

Even the Bahamian defense forces got into the chase. Tommy Turnquest, the national security minister of the Bahamas, said his forces were working with U.S. agents to track down the now international fugitive. "If he is there to be caught our police will catch him," he said.

But Colton slipped away once again. A boat was reported stolen from Great Abaco Island and later spotted on Eleuthera, another island about forty miles to the south. The 44-foot powerboat was taken in Marsh Harbour from the Conch Inn Hotel & Marina. The dock would have been filled with boats. It's the Bahamian home base for The Moorings, a major charter boat operator. Harry Mountain, the hotel's manager, confirmed the theft.

Adding to the suspicion that Colton was behind the theft, the Conch Inn marina is next door to the Curly Tails pub, where Colton was seen on surveillance tape.

After the crash in the mangrove swamp, nearly everything of value from the interior of Miller's plane was removed. Miller expected it would be returned, including four $1,000 headsets. He had received an inventory of the crashed plane's contents from Bahamian officials. When a package arrived from the Bahamas, Miller was stunned that the headsets and other valuables were missing. He accused the Bahamian police of pocketing the valuables Colton had left behind. Miller called it the second theft. "The stealing never stopped," he said. "They returned everything that had no value and kept everything that had value. So who's the thief?"

If Colton caused the first theft and the Bahamians the second theft, Miller's third theft came when he filed his insurance claim. "The insurance company read my policy and started in on me," Miller said. Miller couldn't fight Colton, he wasn't about to start with the Bahamians, but he decided to take on the insurance company. He fought, but it was a losing battle. He reached a settlement.

"I didn't get what I thought I should," Miller said. "That's the way life is."

CHAPTER FIFTY-FOUR

With Colton on the run, the Barefoot Bandit became a sensation in the Bahamas. Bartenders invented drinks in his honor, and the restaurants he broke into publicized his illicit visits to attract customers.

Within days of his getaway from Abaco to Eleuthera, a ferryboat captain spied the tall white man washing in a stream. Then reports started to flood in of Colton sightings. One group of kids said they saw the Barefoot Bandit in a boat and gave chase, to no avail. By the end of the week, experts were predicting that the cat-and-mouse game Colton was playing would soon end. His capture seemed imminent.

"The smell of the end is coming and hopefully it will be a good end and not a bad end," Island County sheriff's detective Ed Wallace said. The crime spree by this point had passed the $3 million mark in stolen and damaged property.

Colton's behavior was changing. Although the pattern was similar, the fugitive seemed to be moving faster. He wasn't trying to cover his tracks as much as he had in the past. "The part that scares me," Wallace said, "is that he seems to be getting grander and grander and less concerned with concealing his identity."

Colton was seen on surveillance video breaking into bars, stealing beer and hunting for food and cash. "What will generally happen, at some point he'll feel so invincible and unstoppable he won't be so careful," said James Alan Fox, an expert criminologist who teaches at Northeastern University in Boston. "He may get complacent. When that will happen, who knows?"

Fox believed that Colton was enjoying the romanticism of his adventures. The crimes were becoming easier to commit and Colton may have thought that the police were no match for his skills. Colton reportedly shouted to a group of islanders that he was bored. He wanted the police to chase him.

"When you start cutting corners, it can ultimately lead to [your] capture," Fox said.

Officials believed they had a good take on Colton's behavior. They knew his M.O. all too well. Whether Colton would surrender or go down fighting, no one knew. Ed Wallace, the detective who had worked Colton's case for eight years, didn't think the story would end simply.

"I don't see him going quietly off into the sunset," Wallace said.

CHAPTER FIFTY-FIVE

Romora Bay Resort and Marina on Harbour Island is an idyllic spot. The rich and famous tie their luxury yachts to the pilings in one of the dock's forty slips. Included in the moorage fee are electric hookups, access to high-speed Internet and use of the gorgeous resort facilities.

The two-year-old resort is posh and frequently attracts celebrities, movie stars and fashion models visiting from Miami, said Kenny Strachan, the resort's security director. Rooms cost more than $400 a night.

Harbour Island, also called Briland by the locals, is about two miles east of Eleuthera, about two hundred miles from Miami. It's a sliver of sand, less than four miles long and no wider than one and a half miles. Although it once was the capital of the Bahamas, today its population is smaller than most inner-city high schools, topping out at no more than two thousand residents. The island is known for its pink sand beaches and world-class scuba diving, and since the early morning hours of July 10, 2010, as the place where the Barefoot Bandit was arrested.

Strachan started his shift that night around 6 p.m. Later that night, after relaxing for a bit in a chair in the lobby, Strachan, fifty-four, decided to stretch his legs. He walked out toward the shimmering infinity pool. Now it was around 11:30 p.m. and a noise out by the marina caught his attention.

"I see this individual hop out of a ten-foot Boston Whaler," Strachan said. "He came running toward me." The security guard recognized Colton. The fugitive's photo was on a wanted poster fixed to the window of the harbormaster's office.

"They're trying to kill me," Strachan remembers Colton saying. The tall, lanky man was running, barefoot, and carrying a pistol in his right hand. Strachan tried to keep pace, tried to tell Colton he could help, but Colton kept running. Strachan stopped the chase. He reached into his pocket and used his cell phone to call the police. It was a fateful call. "I was the one who really informed the police," Strachan said. "I was real proud of that."

The cops arrived within fifteen minutes and spent the next several hours searching for signs of the fugitive. They closed off the area, leaving only the ocean as an escape route.

"After it had been so long, around 2:30 a.m., we heard a boat start up in the marina," Strachan remembered. "The boat just took off with such speed, everyone shouted, 'That's him.' "

Colton throttled the engines on a 32-foot Intrepid, a small, sleek motorboat. The cops were without a boat, so a group of men on the dock offered the police a ride. Heavily armed police jumped into the boat and gave chase.

About a quarter-mile from the marina, Colton's luck ran out. A sandbar helped accomplish what scores of cops couldn't do. Colton ran aground.

Strachan wasn't on the apprehension team, but he heard what happened. As the police approached, they blasted a spotlight at Colton. In response, Colton held the pistol to his head. Colton was yelling at the police not to come closer. He threatened to kill himself, the only alternative the fugitive could think of to avoid going back to jail.

Then the tide began to offer a different way out. The stolen boat began to wiggle free from the sandbar. Police realized then that they had a choice: hold their fire and let Colton continue his spree or let loose a barrage of bullets to immobilize his boat. "If he gets off, they can't catch him," Strachan said. Colton's stolen ride had more horsepower than the cops' borrowed boat. There were a dozen men in the chase boat. Colton was solo and could skim the surface of the water.

The sound of gunfire ripped through the night. The cops opened fire, taking out the twin outboard engines, riddling them with bullet holes.

Now all Colton could do was duck and cover. With the boat damaged, there was nowhere for Colton to run, nowhere to hide. He was cornered. The cat had caught the mouse.

Colton realized the Bahamians might not play by the rules the way the cops in the United States did. They might shoot him. They might actually kill him. "These guys are not going to play games with me," Colton likely thought, said Ed Wallace, the Island County detective. "He had to realize his world was coming to an end."

Wallace believes that Colton saw a stark reality as bullets showered his getaway boat. "He finally realized he didn't live up to his own image." He had a bunch of Bahamians pointing guns at him. His boat was immobilized. He had nowhere to go. He may have been barefoot, but he was a bandit no longer. His wings were broken; he had no place to fly. "He was just Colton from Camano Island," Wallace said.

Before he surrendered, Colton reportedly tossed key evidence into the water, including a computer, the pistol and a cell phone. Investigators haven't said if they've been able to retrieve any useful information from discarded electronics. Salt water is known to be extremely corrosive on electronics.

Colton was in handcuffs for the first time in more than two years. He told his captors they should have killed him.

The Bahamians had snared the Barefoot Bandit.

Back on shore the mood was ecstatic. Despite the early hour, around 3 a.m., word quickly spread that the Barefoot Bandit was captured. Crowds gathered at the dock to catch a glimpse of the infamous fugitive.

"It was extraordinary excitement to bring him back," Strachan said. "They caught him." Months after the incident, the security guard still can't quite believe it all went down at this remote luxury resort. "He was caught here, a few feet away from Romora Bay. He was rushed back into the police hands," he said.

So much had been hyped up about the Bandit. The FBI and dozens of cops had been chasing him all across the United States, all unsuccessfully. Global media had descended on the Bahamas in a frenzy of activity. Now it was over, and Strachan was rightfully proud of the role he played.

"Other people spotted him. They just said they saw him. I made an instant phone call," he said. "I was very excited over that. I felt like I did a good, good, good thing."

To Strachan it wasn't just a matter of personal pride; it was a great moment for the Bahamas. "We do it for the country," he said.

CHAPTER FIFTY-SIX

Bev Davis, the neighbor from Camano Island who wrote the supportive and impassioned e-mail to Colton when he was fifteen and living on the run, wrote another letter, this one to the editor of the *Herald*. It was published in the paper the day news spread of Colton's capture.

Davis raised questions about Colton's father, and why he wasn't being subjected to the media scrutiny that was facing Pam Kohler. "Colt's mother has been hounded, harassed, invaded and lied to by both the police and the media. She has been vilified, ridiculed and belittled," Davis wrote.

She called the reporting biased and unfair. "Seems to me it's almost always bad 'mothering' that takes the blame. What about the 'fathers' in this and other stories where a child goes wrong?" Davis said. "I'd like to know what the 'father' has to say!"

Kohler told me she didn't know where Gordon Moore was. Like other reporters I had tried to track the man down without success.

The media interest in this case was so high that I had producers from national morning television shows calling me at all hours. The producers wanted me to share phone numbers of sources close to Colton. One producer offered to pay for people to stay in a fancy Seattle hotel so that they'd be rested and ready to appear on national television at 4:15 a.m. Pacific time.

The story of the Barefoot Bandit was huge news. Reporters and producers from around the world were interested.

And yet no one turned up Gordon Moore.

Word of Colton's capture spread quickly throughout the Pacific Northwest. People on Camano Island and around the region were elated and relieved. "I am thankful that Colton Harris-Moore has been taken into custody by the Bahamian authorities," Sheriff Mark Brown said. "I pledge my commitment to seek accountability for the many crimes suffered by the citizens of Island County at the hands of this criminal."

Josh Flickner talked to a group of reporters outside the grocery store he manages on Camano Island, steps away from where Colton crashed the Mercedes into a propane tank two year earlier. "I guarantee that our community and that sane people around the country who aren't worshiping him are all feeling really good right now," he said. Flickner used the opportunity to lash out at Colton's fans. "It's disgusting. I think our society worshiping him is just sad. He's nothing more than a thief who's hurt people psychologically, emotionally."

Others had mixed emotions. "We're all very relieved. We're happy he didn't get hurt," said Diana Anderson, a Camano Island resident.

Jason Kersten, a writer who profiled Colton in *Rolling Stone*, wrote a kind of eulogistic postscript on the magazine's Web site. "The greater good has been served, but there was an emptiness in my stomach on Sunday when I heard the news," he said. "I'd be lying if I said there wasn't a part of me that cheered each time he got away."

Like so many people, the end of Colton's run meant the end of the antihero. No more Tweets. No more opportunities to watch Colton fly, or snub his nose at the cops. His turn as the country's trickster was over.

One Camano Island resident told me, “It was fun while it lasted.” But Colton’s running needed to end, the man said.

Colton survived a one-thousand-mile plane ride. He walked away from his fifth plane crash. He was arrested, uninjured, in a hail of bullets. But his mother, Pam Kohler, had nothing to say. “No comment. No, no, no,” she said.

CHAPTER FIFTY-SEVEN

After his arrest, Colton was whisked away on a small plane to Nassau, the capital of the Commonwealth of the Bahamas. Some people feared Colton would get tossed into Fox Hill Prison, the country's only prison. Although the prison was built in 1953 to hold 450 inmates, the population today is much higher, according to the U.S. State Department. It has the reputation of being an awful place, with allegations of abuse by prison guards. Colton avoided Fox Hill altogether. He was held in a cell at the police station.

A snippet of video footage shows Colton with Bahamian police shortly after his arrest. In the footage, investigators ask Colton where he got the gun and he claims he can't remember. He mostly sits quietly, at times sharing a smile with his captors. One man examines Colton's bare feet.

Colton didn't look scared in the clip. He looked tired and desperately thin. He looked pissed off and after several minutes of being filmed said, "Get that camera out of my face."

When the Bahamians went through Colton's possessions, they found his Boy Scout certificate from 1999 recognizing Colton for completing a Cub Scout program. There also were several drawings of airplanes. It's a touching thought to believe that an achievement from when he was eight years old would hold enough value for the fugitive that he would carry it with him for thousands of miles. Police also found a Walther PPK handgun, a weapon made famous in Ian Fleming's James Bond novels.

Colton didn't call his mom from a Bahamian jail cell. It could be that Colton didn't know Kohler's number since she'd changed it several times. Instead, he called Sandy Puttmann, Pam Kohler's sister.

Colton was understandably upset, Puttmann told me.

"Well, of course," she said. Colton's aunt was furious with the media over the way Colton was portrayed. She repeated her rant against the system. She blamed Stanwood School officials and the Island County Sheriff's Office for Colton's behavior. "Why didn't they help him instead of arrest him for every little tiny thing? Why didn't they let him in [the library] and read those books and teach him?" Puttmann asked.

She placed blame on officials for failing to take him away from her sister. "Why didn't they take him away from his mother?" she said.

Diplomats from the American consulate in the Bahamas checked on Colton, the prisoner, and reportedly relayed information to Kohler. By this time, John Henry Browne, a prominent Seattle defense attorney, took on the role of spokesman for the case.

Pam Kohler already had retained O. Yale Lewis, an intellectual property and entertainment attorney. Lewis's client roster includes Courtney Love, the family of Jimi Hendrix, Buddy Holly's widow and others. Lewis said he took the case to help Kohler deal with the onslaught of media attention and to sort through movie and book deals being flung at her from Hollywood.

Kohler released a statement through Lewis's office.

"I am very relieved that Colt is now safe and that no one was hurt during his capture," she said. Though she'd yet to speak to her son, she was yearning for the chance to speak to and see him. "It has been over two and a half years since I have seen him, and I miss him terribly. I hope that it will be possible for me to see him sometime soon. However, I don't yet know when that might happen."

Lewis appeared on NBC's *Today Show* and repeated Kohler's story that she'd tried to seek help, unsuccessfully, for Colton. "She asked the system for help," the attorney said. "And didn't get very much."

Although Colton could have faced a litany of charges in the Bahamas including burglary, theft, illegal weapons possession and illegal entry, he instead was dealt with swiftly. Just three days after his arrest, the fugitive made a brief appearance in a Bahamian courtroom. He was wearing a white T-shirt, a bulletproof vest and navy blue shorts. He was barefoot no more. He had on a pair of white tennis shoes with no laces.

The Bahamian authorities walked Colton up and down the street, parading him for news cameras. He hung his head down, but there was no avoiding the lenses. He can be heard on a piece of video talking to officials before they brought him in front of the waiting news cameras. "Let's make this one fast," he said.

Colton entered a guilty plea to a single count of entering the country illegally. The charge carried a $300 fine, which was paid for by the U.S. Embassy.

Monique Gomez, the lawyer who represented Harris-Moore in court, said she was contacted by an anonymous source who asked her to look in on the six-foot, five-inch prisoner. She said she expected to be paid by some of the dozens of people who called her offering support.

She wouldn't disclose exactly what she and Colton discussed

as he was held in a cell at a local police station. "Colton wants to go home," Gomez said. She described her client as a "brilliant young man, highly intelligent, very nice, very personable." She said the prisoner was in good spirits.

During her brief stint representing Colton, Gomez said she barely had time to eat. She was flooded with calls from an international set of reporters. As he was whisked back to the United States, Gomez offered Colton her regards. "I wish him the best and trust that all goes well for him," she said.

Officials brought him to the airport for a short flight to Miami, where he was turned over to the FBI. From there he was taken to a holding cell to await an identity hearing in U.S. courts.

Once in Miami, Colton went before a federal judge for an identity hearing. He was wearing a tan jumpsuit, white socks and plastic sandals. The judge postponed the hearing a couple of days to give Colton time to retain counsel.

Colton told U.S. Magistrate Judge Robert Dube that he believed his mother had hired a lawyer but he didn't know the man's name. "I'd like to speak with my mom first," Colton said. Colton said he last spoke to Kohler "about a week ago."

Two days later, Colton was back in the courtroom in Miami. This time he didn't utter a word. He appeared with Hector Dopico, an assistant federal public defender who stood in for John Henry Browne. Colton waived his rights to a hearing in Miami, essentially clearing the way for his return to Seattle.

Colton then waited in Miami for his next flight. This time he wouldn't be behind the controls and he certainly wouldn't be barefoot. His flight back to Seattle was aboard the Justice Prisoner and Alien Transportation System, or JPATS, one of the largest prisoner transport systems in the world. It's operated by the U.S. Marshals Service and is more commonly known as

"Con Air." As an article written by the Marshals in 2005 points out, these passengers don't get peanuts, can't watch movies and the seat-belt sign stays illuminated for the duration of the flight. Prisoners wear handcuffs, shackles and a belly chain. About 350,000 prisoners fly Con Air each year, and in 2005, the average cost per prisoner was about $1,153. There is no first-class cabin.

For security reasons, the flights operate secretly and officials wouldn't say when the Barefoot Bandit was scheduled to be delivered back to Seattle. It could be weeks, they said. It was not. Colton arrived in Seattle on the afternoon of July 21. Local television news stations had reporters camped out waiting for Con Air to land. Colton was whisked away to the federal detention center in Sea-Tac, Washington.

PART EIGHT
CAPTURED

CHAPTER FIFTY-EIGHT

Once Colton was in federal detention, investigators, for the first time, took impressions of his entire hand, wrists and palms, not just a fresh set of fingerprints. Like the ridges, curves and lines that make fingerprints unique, the lines on the rest of the hand also can be used as evidence. Crime laboratories in nine states and at the FBI needed a complete set of Colton's prints, including the impressions made by his hands, wrists and fingers, to attempt to link him to evidence in nearly one hundred crimes.

State and federal crime laboratories face significant backlogs in processing evidence. The amount of DNA, fingerprints, writing samples, bullet fragments and other materials that requires the close examination of forensic scientists often piles up. Although some evidence is processed on a first-in, first-out basis, most evidence is shuffled around as investigators on the street bring in priority cases. These pressing cases typically involve violent crimes—murders, rapes, assaults—when suspects are on the loose. Linking physical evidence to a suspect can be enough to lock up a person and take him off the streets. Getting Colton's evidence to the front of the evidence line was going to take time. His crimes mostly were not violent, he was in custody, and he waived rights to a speedy indictment.

Colton came back from the Bahamas with a bad cold. His

attorney, John Henry Browne, said the cold was the first time Colton reported being sick since he'd escaped Griffin Home two years earlier.

Within days of returning to Seattle, Colton made a brief appearance in front of a federal judge. So many reporters attended the hearing marshals were forced to open an overflow gallery in another courtroom.

Colton didn't say much during the brief court appearance, but Browne met with reporters afterward. "He wants kids and everybody to understand that what he did was not fun," Browne said. Colton didn't want to be perceived as a role model, the attorney said.

Browne said Colton seemed childlike and immature. The Barefoot Bandit is "really a kid," and found Colton to be "fascinating, intelligent and introspective."

Browne later went on ABC's *Good Morning America*. On national television, the lawyer said Colton didn't have a plan during his years as a fugitive. He simply was frightened and didn't want to go back to jail. "He was sleeping in culverts, in ditches—and on occasion in a Porta-Potty or two," Browne said.

Now Colton was sleeping in the federal detention center near Seattle's airport. He reportedly was kept in isolation. Federal rules limited his visitors to immediate family and attorneys only. Colton's fan sites on the Internet posted the mailing address so people could send him notes.

Nothing was going to move quickly for Colton. He was arrested on a single federal charge, the Bonners Ferry plane theft. During his initial court appearance in Seattle, Colton waived his opportunity to question his incarceration by the federal government. Browne pointed out that even if the federal government released Colton, he would have been relinquished to one of the other jurisdictions where he faced charges. Or he could have been handed back to the Washington Juvenile Rehabilitation Administration. After all, Colton still owed two years on the sentence from which he absconded in April 2008.

The criminal cases against Colton are extremely complex.

Several factors are at play. Colton's crime spree extended through counties in nine states. He crossed state lines and allegedly committed federal offenses in multiple federal jurisdictions. Colton faced possible prosecution in every jurisdiction where he broke the law. "These are not mutually exclusive prosecutions," said Robert Weisberg, a criminal law expert who teaches at Stanford Law School and is codirector of the Stanford Criminal Justice Center.

Federal prosecutors said that they would attempt to work toward some kind of global resolution of the cases against Colton, but they admitted that achieving a global resolution is difficult. Local prosecutors have the power and right to try whomever they please. Many district attorneys or state prosecutors are elected officials. They could face unhappy constituents if they dismissed cases against a high-profile defendant such as Colton. An equal number of voters may believe prosecutors' time should not be wasted trying redundant offenses against Colton.

Greg Banks, the prosecutor in Island County, where Colton is from, is one prosecutor who said he'd like to bring Colton back and press charges. "He's an Island County problem that ended up causing problems elsewhere," Banks said in October 2010. Colton faces ten criminal counts in Island County stemming from the 2008 crime spree there, including stealing Carol Star's Mercedes. In Madison County, Nebraska, prosecutor Joe Smith said he's patiently waiting to begin proceedings against the infamous suspect. "We're waiting in line for our turn," he said. Prosecutors in San Juan County shared a similar sentiment. Just before Thanksgiving 2010, Skagit County prosecutors filed two felony charges in connection with the February airplane theft in Anacortes.

Each prosecution likely would bring a media circus. In the scenic, small town of Coupeville, on Whidbey Island, Island County officials have begun making contingency plans to accommodate crowds at a possible Colton trial. The county courthouse has only two small courtrooms, each with small galleries. Banks, the prosecutor, said accommodating the national media is just one of the challenges in bringing Colton's cases to trial.

Multiple prosecutions in different courtrooms can exhaust witnesses, especially victims, experts say. The cases are costly both to the government and to the defense. And at some point, judges could agree that adding years to Colton's sentences, if he's convicted, wouldn't lead to his rehabilitation, or would not adhere to the sentencing guidelines set by state and federal statutes.

In November 2010, a federal grand jury handed down a five-count indictment. The feds charged Colton in connection with taking Pat Gardiner's plane from Bonners Ferry, Idaho. That's the plane he allegedly crashed in the clear-cut outside Granite Falls, Washington. He was charged with the ten-minute flight from Anacortes to Eastsound on February 10, 2010. He allegedly piloted the plane without an airman's certificate, a violation of federal law. Two federal counts were related to stolen firearms, including being a fugitive in possession of a firearm. The fifth count charged Colton with sailing the boat across the Columbia River from Washington to Oregon.

Appearing in court on November 18, 2010, Colton entered a not guilty plea. A trial date was set for early January 2011, but the date was expected to slip. Emily Langlie, a spokeswoman for the U.S. Attorney's Office in Seattle, said prosecutors may amend charges at any time. That means Colton could face additional federal charges as more evidence is collected. (Indeed, the trial date was set over until July 11, 2011, a year to the day since Colton's arrest in the Bahamas. Both prosecutors and attorneys for Colton said they needed more time to prepare the case for either a jury trial or a plea agreement.)

The most serious charge Colton faces in Island County carries a maximum sentence of seven years, Banks said. Most often, criminals convicted in property crimes cases are ordered to serve concurrent sentences, not consecutive, or back-to-back, sentences. Judges in Washington State have some flexibility to add months or years to the sentence if prosecutors can prove aggravating factors. Banks said he believed it would be appropriate to ask a judge to find aggravating factors in Colton's cases. Aggravating factors in property crimes include recent recidivism and a high offender score. Offender scores are calculated based on criminal history. Colton would have a very high offender score, Banks said.

Prosecutors already have disclosed in court papers a number of cases where Colton left evidence at crime scenes. Another factor weighing against the defendant is prosecutors' ability to use certain circumstantial evidence against Colton. Ordinarily, it's hard to prove a case based on a criminal's pattern or M.O., Banks said. Colton's cases may be an exception. Banks said he could argue that Colton repeated a pattern dozens of times. The sheer volume of the cases weighs heavily on the defendant.

A fingerprint on a stolen car in Cody, Wyoming, in and of itself, may not seem like enough evidence to bring about a conviction, but the collected circumstantial evidence of Colton's pattern likely could sway a jury. Whether circumstantial evidence could be admitted, "ultimately that will be a question for a judge to determine," Banks said.

When Colton made a brief appearance in federal court in Seattle in July, he waived his right to a detention hearing. He could have asked the judge to release him. Prosecutors laid out their argument for keeping him locked up in an eight-page memorandum to the judge. He was called an "extreme" flight risk and a danger to society. While sometimes suspects can be released to relatives, the feds pointed out that Colton's closest relative, Pam Kohler, wasn't to be trusted. She'd already been quoted worldwide encouraging him to flee the country to a place with no extradition treaty with the United States.

A reporter asked John Henry Browne why he hadn't argued for Colton to be released on bail. Browne did a double take. The lawyer fired back a question of his own: "Do you live around here?" It seemed improbable to free a suspect who'd just spent two years running top speed from police.

Most experts agree that wherever Colton faces prosecution, the cases will not proceed to a jury. Instead the cases will be resolved in deals made between Colton's attorneys and prosecutors. At Colton's arraignment in federal court, Browne confirmed he was working toward a plea deal and several prosecutors had already agreed not to file charges against Colton.

Legal experts believe the best defense strategy would be to play up his troubled past and hope for leniency in sentencing. Many legal experts pointed out that Browne's comments on Colton's behalf had to be taken in context. The lawyer was laying the foundation for a defense strategy. Instead of challenging the facts, Colton's defense team is more likely to focus on arguing for a reduced sentence.

"Very little of this will have to do with contesting the charges in conventional legal terms," said Weisberg, the criminal law expert. A strong defense will present many mitigating factors, including Colton's childhood and his tumultuous upbringing. Lawyers may argue that Colton was never given a chance at success, Weisberg said. The strategy probably will not keep Colton out of jail altogether, but it could help limit the number of years he can expect to spend behind bars.

Colton's defense attorneys also must combat the public perception that Colton publicized his wrongdoing, said Mary D. Fan, a professor at the University of Washington School of Law in Seattle. She's also a former federal prosecutor. Browne's public comments on the case seem to be downplaying Colton's behavior.

"We're almost getting a preview of a sentencing," Fan said. "The defense is already saying, 'Judge, we're not glorifying the commission of crimes.' "

Andrew Vachss, the nationally known attorney and child advocate, believes Colton's defense attorney likely would build a defense that is based on both his psychiatric and social profile. Sometimes, especially with defendants where there is an abundance of evidence that could prove someone's guilt, a lawyer's job is to convince a judge or jury that their client had little choice, that "he was a desperate, lost person seeking a way to find his way in the world with no guide." Vachss isn't sure that is true for Colton. The lawyer would have to spend hours interviewing the defendants to be certain.

However the cases are adjudicated, Colton is expected to serve many years behind bars. Experts said that guessing how judges will take into account all his crimes, his prior convictions, and his escape is an open question. As of this book's printing, it seemed likely that Colton was going to stay locked up for at least a decade. That would make him around thirty years old at the time of his release.

Browne speculated his client would serve no more than a dozen years, likely less. A reporter asked him if Colton could be put away for decades. Browne said that was impossible. "That will never happen because he has a really good lawyer."

When I asked Kohler what she thought about the prospect of Colton spending a decade behind bars, she said, "Oh, well. I don't know what to say." Six months after Colton's arrest, Kohler had yet to visit him in the detention center, eighty-two miles from her home. "I don't drive that far," she said. "I can see him, it's just that I don't drive that far." Even if she made the trip, she couldn't see him in person. He'd speak to her via a closed-circuit television connection.

Kohler said she traded letters with him and he was allowed to call her once a month. "It sounds like he's fine. He don't particularly care for where he's at." Colton told his lawyer he preferred to remain in isolation as he awaited the outcome of his federal trial. He spent his time reading magazines, including a gift subscription from his mother to *National Geographic*. Colton drew pictures of airplanes and he sketched a new design for his mother's garden. He flipped through catalogues for the outdoors store Cabela's and read fan mail. A group of students in France studied his case as a project for English class and mailed him their papers.

A question that has surfaced is whether Colton or his mom could profit from his story. Federal law and the laws of Washington State prohibit people convicted of violent crimes from profiting by way of sharing their stories. The provisions are called "Son of Sam" laws, named for the serial killer David Berkowitz. People didn't want Berkowitz, whose rampage terrorized New York City in the late 1970s, to make a fortune by selling his story. Laws were passed to prevent such a windfall.

But Colton wasn't known to be violent, hasn't been charged with any violent crimes and has no convictions that would meet the standard for the state's "Son of Sam" law. It doesn't mean that Colton, or his mother, could be prevented by law from cashing in on his exploits.

Federal prosecutors could structure a plea arrangement that would prohibit Colton from selling the story. When another infamous teenage criminal, the so-called American Taliban, John Walker Lindh, pleaded guilty in 2002 to helping the Taliban, he was sentenced to twenty years behind bars. Lindh also agreed to forfeit any money he made from a book or movie deal to the federal government. The restriction extended to Lindh's friends or relatives. There's a good chance the prosecutors in Colton's case could seek a similar deal. "It certainly is something that prosecutors can consider here," Fan said.

Prosecutors bringing charges against Colton also could try to structure the deal to prevent his mother or other relatives or associates of Colton from profiting. "A smart prosecutor can artfully craft a plea agreement to clamp down on end runs," Fan said.

Jenny A. Durkan, the U.S. Attorney in Seattle, was adamant that Colton's story not be perceived as entertainment. Colton did nothing that deserved admiration or glorification, she said. "Real people were hurt."

Browne told *Good Morning America* just after the arrest in the Bahamas that Colton wasn't interested in making money off his story. "He felt if he told it or gave it away, it would no longer be his story."

Browne said Colton likened it to looking in a mirror and having someone else steal your soul. "It was really interesting," the attorney said. "He's one of the most interesting people I've ever met," Browne said. The prisoner is "smart, but at the same time naïve."

Even so, rumors began to spread among New York publishing houses of a possible first-person account from Colton. In

November Browne said Colton was reconsidering trying to sell the story as a way to earn money toward the hundreds of thousands of dollars in restitution payments and possibly millions of dollars in fines he likely will owe. "He's very reluctant to make a dime off this, he really is," Browne said. Still, Colton changed his mind "a little bit" when he learned paying back victims could reduce his time behind bars.

It was unclear how prosecutors would respond to Colton's effort to earn money by talking about his criminal escapades.

POSTSCRIPT

In the time since Zack Sestak started the Colton Harris-Moore fan page on Facebook, he's been taunted and targeted, criticized for supporting someone so many people believe to be a punk thief. Sestak has received threats and been called names. He's let the negativity roll off him. He defends his actions and said he would not hesitate to do it all over again.

"My heart goes out to Colton; he's a really troubled young man," Sestak said. As he's watched the story blossom, he said he can't help but be upset that Colton may be prevented from getting a share in the inevitable profits from movies, books or other accounts. Instead Colton is "just getting the shit end of the stick, sitting there in federal prison."

Like many other people, Sestak said he would like to hear directly from Colton. He wants to know what it is like to be Colton Harris-Moore, to have a Facebook following, to endure what Colton endured. "I would just be interested and compelled to hear his point of view, and hear his story as seen through his eyes," Sestak said.

Late in October 2010, Sestak offered a new message on the Facebook page he'd created for the Barefoot Bandit. While other people put up posts urging Colton to escape, Sestak offered a more direct approach: "Free Colton."

Colton began stealing as a way to feed himself, to survive.

Along the way, Colton became more sophisticated at stealing identities and slipping away undetected. "He kind of refined it," Mike Rocha, the bounty hunter, said. "He wanted people to know it was him. He wanted to have some notoriety."

Nine months after Colton drew giant footprints in chalk across the floor at Kyle Ater's Orcas Island grocery store, Ater took his girlfriend to Hawaii for a week. It was the first vacation Ater had allowed himself since opening the organic store four years earlier. Just back from his holiday, Ater told me Colton's burglaries felt personal. After police had investigated, Ater said he felt the hair stand up on the back of his neck and had the sense he was being watched. The store owner was certain Colton lurked nearby, peering out at the cops who used high-tech equipment to try to find the hidden Barefoot Bandit. Ater kept having a feeling he was being watched.

And when Colton started to bolt east, Ater said he couldn't believe it. "I thought it was amazing how he managed to get all the way to the Bahamas," Ater said. "There's something about this story that's intriguing. Most people would have blundered one of the burglaries."

Most people would have been caught speeding on a freeway. Most people would have stopped in a big city where an alert police officer might recognize them. Most people would have fallen asleep and been caught off guard. Colton wasn't most people.

For Colton, it was like a video-game addiction, several people said. "He needed to take it up to the next level," Ater said. Colton was playing a sort of real-life version of Grand Theft Auto, except for Colton it was "grand theft boat, auto, plane, bicycle," Ater said. "Where does it start, where does it end?"

Ed Wallace, the Island County detective, pointed out that Colton stole much more than necessities. He took iPods, cameras, gadgets. "He was stealing stuff he wants," Wallace said. "He committed burglaries and ID thefts to get toys for himself." He had to feed the James Bond–like persona he'd imagined for himself. "He had his tastes."

Sheriff Bill Cumming assessed Colton as a bright enough young man. "His intelligence is probably pretty high," the sheriff said. "He uses that in an antisocial way, by committing crimes and creating victims in our community."

What will happen to Colton once he's released from prison? Will he follow his friend Harley Davidson Ironwing and continue to commit crimes, only to be sent back to jail over and over again? Could his ingenuity and cleverness be harnessed? Would the government recruit him, like they did with Frank Abagnale Jr., the con artist and fraudster portrayed in the film *Catch Me If You Can?*

One law enforcement official told me Colton would be perfect for military Special Forces because he seemed to lack any sense of fear. Another person suggested putting his pilot skills to work in the military drone program. The idea of Colton joining the armed services seems a bit far-fetched. Although the military has loosened the rules about convicts qualifying for duty, Colton's lengthy record probably would disqualify him. Colton probably will never qualify as a private pilot, either. The FAA frowns on granting credentials to convicted felons.

Colton forever will wear the mantle he earned as the Barefoot Bandit. Upon release, the prison system probably will dump him back in Island County, where he grew up. Typically prisoners return to their homes, where they're more likely to know people and be able to succeed, officials said.

In Island County, people know Colton.

"A lot of the press coverage glorified him," said Peter

Domoto, the Camano Island man whose Zodiac was taken in 2004. Domoto believes the press attention fueled Colton's ambitions. "The attention he got was probably what fed him. It was kind of like a high for him. He probably was seeking that kind of attention and adulation most of his life."

Domoto doesn't pin all the blame for changes to island living on Colton, though. Colton's crimes heightened awareness, but island living has its advantages and pitfalls. Homes are treasured because they're remote. That same isolation makes them vulnerable to burglaries. "That's island life," Domoto said.

Mostly, Domoto said, he feels sorry for Colton. "I wish that he had gotten help earlier. He's got potential to straighten himself out," he said. "He's obviously not stupid."

Domoto wonders what might have happened if Colton had gotten help after he stole the inflatable dinghy. "Maybe all of this wouldn't have happened," he said. That's a sentiment shared by many people who were victimized by Colton.

Beatrice von Tobel, the airport manager on Orcas Island, isn't alone in her belief that Colton's talent will be wasted if he's incarcerated. "I feel bad that nobody interrupted him earlier," she said. As a former educator and guidance counselor, she believes that Colton could have been put on a better path. Instead, he's well fed and has a place to sleep; he's got "three hots and a cot" in prison, she said. "What more can you want?"

Ater, the grocery store owner, believes even a decade behind bars isn't enough justice for the burglar who nearly forced the organic grocery out of business. "He's outside a normal crime wave," Ater said. He believes that Colton should be forced to pay back all that he stole, and restitution for all the damage he did. But Ater isn't hopeful he'll see much in the way of restitution. If only the cops would return his $350 drill, then "it's not a total loss."

Colton's most daring crime likely also carried the greatest dollar value. Prosecutors likely will focus on Colton's 1,000-mile joyride in John Miller's plane. The plane was valued at around $650,000. Federal and state sentencing guidelines often rely on factors, including property value, to determine the appropriate punishment. For his part, John Miller said he doesn't see justice in putting Colton behind bars.

"Won't serve any purpose to put him in jail," Miller said. Miller believes Colton should be put to work cleaning airplanes to earn the money to repay his victims. "He can't do that while he's in jail. That's what I think," Miller said. "No one will listen to me."

Miller hasn't replaced his Cessna and doesn't believe he will. He has access to a friend's plane, but he isn't flying as much as he had in the past. "The old boy put me on foot. I miss it," Miller said.

Despite the loss of the airplane, Miller said he doesn't harbor animosity toward Colton. "I'm glad the police didn't shoot him, glad he wasn't hurt in my airplane," Miller said. "I'd like to see him rehabilitated. I don't have any desire to see him punished severely. Punishment would be working to repay the damage."

Bev Davis, the neighbor who reached out to Colton, described him as highly intelligent but socially immature. Now she just hopes Colton gets help. "If he gets a life, gets medication, gets reprogrammed, he's got a good shot at some good thing," Davis said. "Who knows what prison will do?"

Davis said she continues to think about him daily. "All I know is, I wish him the very best. I've always loved him and prayed for him and I always will," she said.

Kohler refused to take responsibility for Colton's behavior, blaming the system, doctors, social workers and teachers.

She repeatedly blamed the Island County Sheriff's Office, the school system, the state. Kohler's sister shares in the displacement. They wanted someone else, the system, to fix the boy.

"Society can't fix everything," said Rocha, the bounty hunter.

Colton's lawyer, John Henry Browne, said his client didn't enjoy his time on the run. Colton was scared, hungry and lonely, Browne has been quoted as saying. Colton's actions tell a different story. He committed crimes with a passion, over and over again. He did it with style and with the occasional gloating. There's little doubt that Colton may have at times felt desperate—he must have—but he surely felt thrilled when gunning John Miller's Cessna at more than 200 miles per hour. His adrenaline must have been pumping when he jumped out of Carol Star's Mercedes. Or when he laughed at a San Juan County deputy as he outran the cop and disappeared into the woods. Or when a Black Hawk helicopter sought him near Granite Falls. Or when SWAT teams chased him on the slopes of Turtleback Mountain and on the coast of Orcas Island. Or when he logged on to the Internet and read story after story of his remarkable ability to slip away.

Colton created a kind of spy man, Jason Bourne image for himself. He didn't just steal to survive, but to fulfill his desires. He achieved the American dream the other old-fashioned way: he became a thief. He went farther and faster than his upbringing had prepared him to go through legitimate means. He was the first criminal folk hero of the Internet age, yet his crimes were mostly low-tech. In another age he would have been celebrated in ballads sung around campfires and in saloons. Today those songs have a worldwide audience on the Internet and YouTube. In our era he was celebrated on Facebook and blogs.

He was scolded and celebrated on cable TV. He was a lost kid who found a place in his own era. Colton became a truly American phenomenon.

Yes, Colton had victims. No matter their station or wealth, they deserve restitution. They each felt the pain of violation and loss. Colton's illegally won gains were earned on the backs of people who worked hard. Colton may have been stealing to survive, but to what end? He spent his first decade being abused, his second decade committing crimes, and will probably spend the third decade of his life locked up. That doesn't sound much like survival.

In the end, Andrew Vachss sees in Colton a child with a lot of suffering, needless and avoidable suffering. "This kid hurts and he hurts pretty bad," Vachss said. "I can't see anything that I've ever seen about him that says he deserves to hurt."

A NOTE ABOUT SOURCING

I used a variety of source material to compile this book. Much of the information came from the three years of beat reporting on the case when I wrote more than one hundred stories about Colton Harris-Moore under my byline for the *Herald* of Everett, Washington. This book is much more than a collection of those articles. I found dozens of additional experts, victims and people affected by this extraordinary tale. I reviewed the reams of court documents already filed in cases involving Colton. There also was the work of many other reporters who chased this story. In almost every case in which I used another reporter's work, I tried to re-report the content and reinterview the sources. In my experience, I've found that there are always additional details to learn and more insight to be gained. That was the case with this project as well; however, in some instances it just wasn't possible to reach every person. There are some specific outlets, reporters and stories that provided unmatchable detail.

The history of the Mark Clark Bridge and the gateway to Camano Island relied on an August 12, 2010, story by Gale Fiege that ran in the *Herald*. History of Colton's early life is found in Island and Snohomish counties' court records. Some details came from the profile of the Barefoot Bandit by Jason Kersten that ran in *Rolling Stone* on May 13, 2010. *The Islands' Sounder* reported information about Colton's crime spree on the San Juan Islands that Sheriff Bill Cumming declined to review with me with criminal cases pending. Mike Collins wrote about Colton for the *Aircraft Owners and Pilots Association Pilot Magazine* in the November 2010 issue. His story provided details about the aircraft and interviews with pilots who became Colton's victims. Details of John Henry Browne's career and life were drawn from a profile of the lawyer that ran on March 22, 1998, in the *Seattle Times*. I included some details that producer Paul LaRosa and his team at CBS News unearthed for a *48 Hours Mystery* hour-long special that aired on November 13, 2010. Associated Press reporter Gene Johnson doggedly tracked this story and first explored the possibility of the John Walker Lindh precedent to potentially curb Colton's ability to profit. AP reporters also were on the ground in both the Bahamas and Miami and provided quotes and source information that is contained in the final chapters. Some of Colton's last days of freedom were described in Erik Lacitis's July 26, 2010, story that ran in the *Seattle Times*.

Much of Colton's childhood history was examined in a twelve-page report filed in Island County. Details of his early crimes filled dog-eared files in both Snohomish and Island counties. Federal court papers also provided detail into his more recent alleged criminal activities.

How Colton pulled off his two-year crime spree, how he flew, how he managed on his own may never be known. This account is what we do know. It's grounded in the facts, many the same that police and prosecutors are gathering to hold Colton Harris-Moore accountable for the crimes he allegedly committed.

ACKNOWLEDGMENTS

The author wishes to thank many people who helped make this book possible. Dozens of people gave up their time to talk to me, especially Colton's victims, who never asked to be a part of this story. A special nod also to the men and women in law enforcement who worked hard to bring Colton to justice. A great deal of credit goes to the entire newsroom at the *Herald* of Everett, Washington. I could not have completed this project without the support of Allen Funk and Neal Pattison. My thanks go to all my colleagues at the paper, especially those who were thrust into this story from time to time, including Eric Stevick, Noah Haglund, Kaitlin Manry, Krista Kapralos, Jim Haley, Katya Yefimova and Gale Fiege. Diana Hefley always will be my partner in crime. Graphic artist Judy Stanley fell and broke her heel the morning that Colton was arrested. She never liked Colton much before her fall; she liked him less after. Justin Best and the entire photo staff are awesome. Robert Frank provided his endless enthusiasm. Scott North invested his great mind and incisive critical voice into the hundreds of stories I wrote on his watch. He deserves much credit and thanks.

Sarah Jackson, Theresa Goffredo, Ron Ramey, Sally Birks and Melanie Munk provided tremendous support.

Many people outside the paper deserve mention. Phil Gambone first inspired me to write and still does. Mike and Sandy Thoele, Dean Rea, Tom Maurer, Jerry Casey and Gene Johnson, among others, showed me the journalistic ropes.

Jeanne Sather read the manuscript while she was undergoing cancer treatments. She provided invaluable feedback. The Potter de Haan family is wonderful. Linda Potter is a great fan and line editor. Her daughter, kc, kindly took my portrait; Jac helped with technology. Eliot, who hasn't turned two, provided a boost by saying my name for the first time while I worked on the book.

David Patterson, my agent, believed in me and this project. Mark Chait and NAL took a chance on a first-time author and made this book a reality.

Many more friends and colleagues were supportive of me. Thank you all.

My partner, Jeremy Moser, not only put up with me during the book's writing; he helped read and line-edit the final manuscript. For this, and for so much more, he is the best.

Photo by KC Potter de Haan

Jackson Holtz is an award-winning reporter at the *Herald* of Everett in Washington State. He lives in Seattle with his cat, Emily, and his partner of more than sixteen years, Jeremy Moser.